Jil Caroline Onimus

Assessing the Economic Value of Venture Capital Contracts

GABLER RESEARCH

EBS Forschung

Schriftenreihe der EBS Universität für Wirtschaft und Recht i. Gr.
EBS Business School · Wiesbaden

Herausgegeben von
Prof. Dr. Falko Fecht

Band 78

Die im Sommer 2010 aus der European Business School International University, Schloss Reichartshausen entstandene EBS Universität für Wirtschaft und Recht (i. Gr.) gGmbH ist die erste Wirtschaftsuniversität in Deutschland. Dieser Vorreiterrolle fühlen sich ihre Professoren und Doktoranden in Forschung und Lehre verpflichtet. Mit der Schriftenreihe präsentiert die EBS Universität für Wirtschaft und Recht i. Gr. ausgewählte Ergebnisse ihrer betriebs- und volkswirtschaftlichen Forschung.

Jil Caroline Onimus

Assessing the Economic Value of Venture Capital Contracts

An Option Pricing Approach

GABLER

RESEARCH

Bibliographic information published by the Deutsche Nationalbibliothek
The Deutsche Nationalbibliothek lists this publication in the Deutsche Nationalbibliografie; detailed bibliographic data are available in the Internet at http://dnb.d-nb.de.

Dissertation EBS Universität für Wirtschaft und Recht i. Gr. | EBS Business School | Wiesbaden, 2010

D 1540

1st Edition 2011

Editorial Office: Stefanie Brich | Britta Göhrisch-Radmacher

Gabler Verlag is a brand of Springer Fachmedien.
Springer Fachmedien is part of Springer Science+Business Media.
www.gabler.de

Cover design: KünkelLopka Medienentwicklung, Heidelberg
Printed on acid-free paper
Printed in Germany

ISBN 978-3-8349-2812-2

Acknowledgments

Any specialist of contingent claims analyzing a VC contract would be struck by the frequency of conditional sentences, which hint at the presence of real options. Although I was not a real options specialist at the outset of my thesis, this observation rang a bell and helped me identify a nascent and promising strand of research: the pricing of VC contracts using real options analysis.

I then discovered that the existing research in this field focuses on only some of the contractual terms, instead of covering the entire contract, and does not account for the fact that most contract terms are "triggered" by future events (such as follow-on VC financings or exit events). Had it not been attempted to expand the scope of analysis, or was it methodologically infeasible to do so? I strongly feared that the latter explanation was more likely, but believed it was worth an attempt. I started building a "comprehensive" pricing model, that would cover the majority of standard terms and account for interaction effects as well as trigger events.

If this challenging attempt had a successful end, this is to a large extent due to the support I was given by academics and practitioners, as well as close friends and family.

First of all, I would like to thank my advisors, Prof. Dr. Lutz Johanning (Professor of Empirical Capital Market Research at WHU, Otto Beisheim School of Management) and Prof. Dr. Gerhard Picot (Founder and Senior Partner at the German law firm PICOT Rechtsanwaltsgesellschaft mbH), for their ongoing support and patience throughout the evolution of the project. Prof. Dr. Lutz Johanning helped me delimit the research topic and shape the empirical part of the analysis. Prof. Dr. Gerhard Picot consistently challenged me with questions from a practitioner's perspective and supported my efforts to bridge the gap between theoretical research and contracting practice.

The contract pricing model derived in this thesis would be a pure academic exercise, were it not based on insights from experts on VC contracting and empirical data on VC transactions. Therefore, I am grateful to Fenwick & West LLP for granting me access to the dataset underlying its report on "Trends in Terms of Venture Financings in Silicon Valley", recognized as a report of reference to the VC industry. I am especially indebted to the authors of this report, Michael Patrick and Barry Kramer (Partners of Fenwick & West's Corporate Group), who helped me in a series of interviews to evaluate the dataset and interpret the results.

I am also very grateful to Hassan Sohbi, Partner at Taylor Wessing LLP (Frankfurt), for his personal introductions, notably to the Fenwick & West team in California, and for sharing his expertise in VC contracting practices in Europe and differences as compared to the U.S.

Furthermore, I am thankful to Alain Razakarivony, my friend and former colleague, for his support in programming the software application and solving methodological issues. His expertise and ideas saved me considerable time and effort.

I have a profound debt to my family, who has encouraged me over the years and respected my academic ambitions, even though the realization of these ambitions required substantial concessions in other dimensions of life. They refrained from declaring me as a computer nerd when I ran simulations during dinners, or when I monopolized server capacities in their offices. They shared the hard times and they shared the euphoria at the end of the journey.

My deepest gratitude goes to Curt Gunsenheimer, my boyfriend, occasional scientific co-author and full-fledged Venture Capitalist. He provided me with intellectual support and practitioner insights for the thesis, while cultivating our relationship on a day-to-day basis. Since it is very hard to find more unromantic topics than venture capital contracting paired with real options, he has surely paid a very high price for the option to expand our relationship over time. I intend to compensate for his efforts in the next phase of our lives, which starts right with the publication of this book!

Paris, November 2010 Jil C. Onimus

Contents

List of Figures

List of Tables

1 Introduction

1.1 Problem Definition

Venture Capital (VC) is a segment of the private equity industry, which focuses on investing in new companies with high growth potential and accompanying high risk. This risk profile of such investments is related to high market and technology uncertainties as well as high information asymmetry and agency cost between VC investors and company management. In this uncertain environment, it is not possible for VC investors to predict with reasonable certainty the future performance of an investee company and to derive a reliable estimate of company value at the outset of the investment. Instead, investors address this issue by designing and negotiating complex investment contracts. These contracts provide them with information and management rights to actively monitor and influence the investee company's performance as well as with decision rights related to future corporate events (see Klausner, 2001; Sahlman, 1990; Schertler, 2001).

The academic literature on the design of VC contracts has shed considerable light on the structure and function of these agreements, initially focusing on the U.S. market only and increasingly expanding the scope of analysis to other countries. Research has been hampered by the lack of data availability (given the private nature of VC investments) and by the heterogeneity of VC practices across countries, specifically in terms of contract design. The combinations of terms used and their specification vary substantially across countries, since they are adapted to the specific institutional and regulatory frameworks. Theoretical research on optimal contract design traditionally takes on a *functional* perspective. It derives optimal incentive and control structures that mitigate the information asymmetry and agency problems between the VC investors and company management and translates these structures into specific financial instruments and legal provisions applicable for different countries.[1] Empirical studies on VC contracting practices, on the other hand, take on a *formal* approach. They analyze the choice and specification of terms used in different countries and mirror their findings with the theoretical predictions.[2] This traditional focus on *form* and *function* brings about major difficulties. First, optimality arguments cannot be derived on a general basis, but must be derived and validated individually for each country, since a specific function may be fulfilled by different forms in different countries. This explains that empirical findings in European countries are not fully aligned with the theoretical predictions developed in the U.S.

1 Theoretical studies include, among others, Bergemann & Hege (1998, 2000), Admati & Pfleiderer (1994), Nöldeke & Schmidt (1998), Bascha & Walz (2001).

2 Empirical findings are presented, for example, in Gompers (1995), Kaplan & Strömberg (2002a, 2002b), Lerner (1994), or Gompers & Lerner (1996a).

(see Jung-Senssfelder, 2006, pp. 44-45; Schertler, 2000, p. 17). Secondly, the existing approaches cannot address the full complexity of interactions among individual terms and of the shared ownership of rights between parties (see Cossin, 2002).

Neither theoretical nor empirical research on VC contract design accounts for the *economic value* of contract terms, although this approach is widely used in the literature covering other types of financing agreements such as debt contracts or joint venture agreements.[3] It has been shown that the terms of contractual agreements generate exotic options that can be priced using advanced option pricing techniques such as Monte Carlo simulation with probability distribution modeling (see Ashkeboussi, Juan and Olmos, 2007). For VC contracts, this *economic value* approach is still in a nascent stage. Woronoff and Rosen (2005a) show that VC contract terms can significantly affect the distribution of value among the parties upon exit, and should therefore be quantified at the outset of the investment. They suggest to capture the economic value of terms indirectly, by accounting for their influence on the expected distribution of payoffs among the parties at exit. However, they do not employ asset pricing techniques to quantify this effect. Chemla, Habib and Ljungqvist (2004) analyze shareholder agreements in general and find that the major clauses in these agreements can be interpreted as options, whether they represent explicit options (as in the case of put and call clauses), or implicit options (as in the case of drag-

3 See Merton (1974), Ingersoll (1977), Black & Cox (1976), and Anderson & Sundaresan (1996).

along rights or catch-up clauses). In their study, the real option approach is essentially used to gain a better understanding of incentive and control mechanisms, but not to assess the economic value of contract features. The first systematic analysis of VC contract values based on option pricing is performed by Cossin, Leleux and Saliasi (2002). Their framework addresses some of the major covenants found in VC contracts (i.e. liquidation preference, staging, conversion and anti-dilution) and shows how they can be priced in interaction, using closed-form solutions and numerical analysis (based on finite differences). However, it excludes various provisions used in practice (such as voting rights, drag-along rights or redemption rights) and does not account for the fact that provisions become exercisable upon future events such as share issues or exit transactions. Finally, the analysis is performed in a setting with a single investor and a single series of preferred shares, which does not reflect the reality of VC financings.

To the author's best knowledge, there is no comprehensive model of VC contract pricing, which covers the majority of provisions used in practice and accounts for interaction effects and shared ownership of rights, in a realistic setting with several investors and multiple financing rounds. When practitioners make trade-offs on individual contract terms, they rely on "rule of thumb" estimates, since they have no tool at hand to measure the value of such terms.

1.2 Research Objectives

This thesis develops an option pricing model for the valuation of VC investment contracts. The model follows a comprehensive approach, covering all major provisions of such contracts and accounting for interaction effects between these various provisions. It also accommodates multiple rounds with multiple option holders (VC investors).

The real option values derived from the model correspond to the economic values of entire contracts. By comparing the values of alternative contracts with different combinations of terms, it is possible to obtain the value of individual terms in their interactions. The pricing methodology is based on Least Squares Monte Carlo simulation and flexible enough to account for the specificities of options embedded in VC contracts such as trigger events, jumps in the underlying asset path and shared option ownership.

The analysis focuses specifically on VC contracting practices in the U.S. market, which represents the largest and oldest VC market worldwide. Accordingly, it relies on model legal documents published by the U.S. National Venture Capital Association (NVCA) to identify standard contract terms and on time series data on VC investments performed in the U.S. to specify the parameters of the model. However, this geographic focus on the U.S. market does not affect the general applicability of the model, since the latter can be adapted to contracting practices in other countries by using local model contracts and time series data.

In order to obtain numerical estimates of contract values, the author provides an application of the pricing model to standard investment scenarios, which reflect different degrees of contractual protection for the investor. This work aims at contributing to several streams of academic research. First, it extends the nascent research line on the economic value of VC contracts along multiple dimensions: (a) by broadening the range of legal terms covered to include the majority of terms, (b) by accounting for the complex interaction effects between these terms, (c) by providing numerical estimates of the economic value of contracts, (d) by applying a novel option pricing technique to this research line. Secondly, this contract pricing model can be used to add an economic value dimension to the theoretical and empirical analysis of VC contract design.

1.3 Definitions

The definitions provided in this section are adapted to the specific context of this thesis, that is the pricing of options embedded in VC contracts. Therefore, they draw from a number of distinct fields of research and practice, notably from financial and real option pricing, VC contract design as well as legal language used by practitioners in the structuring of VC deals.

1.3.1 General Venture Capital Terms

1.3.1.1 Venture Capital Investors

The definition of *VC investors* used in this study is closely aligned with the definition of "VC firms" provided in the NVCA Yearbook 2009 (see Thomson Reuters [TR], 2009, p. 18). It covers VC firms investing through *limited partnerships* with *fixed commitment levels* and *fixed lives* and does not include infinite lived "evergreen funds" [4] or captive corporate industrial investment groups without fixed commitment levels.

VC firms can be categorized as follows:

- *Private independent firms*: independent private and public firms including both institutionally and non-institutionally funded firms and family groups.
- *Financial institutions*: firms that are affiliates or subsidiaries of investment banks and non-investment bank financial entities including commercial banks and insurance companies.
- *Corporations*: VC subsidiaries and affiliates of industrial corporations.
- *Other entities*: Any firm meeting the above criteria and not included in the three former categories.

[4] This term refers to funds that have a continuous infusion of capital from a parent organization as opposed to the fixed life and commitment level of closed-end VC funds.

Accordingly, the definition does not include *Business Angels* (or Business Angel Networks), who represent wealthy individuals (or groups of such individuals) investing their private capital in early-stage companies, with different investment strategies and contracting practices than those of VC investors analyzed in this thesis.

1.3.1.2 Venture Capital Financing

Venture Capital is a segment of the private equity industry (alongside the second major segment of Buyouts), which focuses on investing in new companies with high growth potential and accompanying high risk. VC financings can be categorized along the following stages (see TR, 2009, pp. 87-88):

1. Seed or start-up financing: This stage is a relatively small amount of capital provided to an inventor or entrepreneur to prove a concept. This involves product development and market research as well as building a management team and developing a business plan (if the initial steps are successful). This is a pre-marketing stage.

2. Early stage financing: This stage provides financing to companies completing development where products are mostly in testing or pilot production. In some cases, products may have just been made commercially available. Companies may be in the process of organizing or they may already be in business for three years or less. Usually such firms will have made market studies, assembled the

key management, developed a business plan, and are ready or have already started conducting business.

3. Expansion stage financing: This stage involves working capital for the initial expansion of a company that is producing and shipping and has growing accounts receivables and inventories. It may or may not be showing a profit. Some of the uses of capital may include further plant expansion, marketing, working capital, or development of an improved product. More institutional investors are more likely to be included along with initial investors from previous rounds. The VC investor's role in this stage evolves from a supportive role to a more strategic role.

4. Later stage financing: Capital in this stage is provided for companies that have reached a fairly stable growth rate; that is, not growing as fast as the rates attained in the expansion stages. Again, these companies may or may not be profitable and cash-flow positive, but are more likely to be than in previous stages of development. This also includes companies considering an Initial Public Offering (IPO).

5. Bridge financing: temporary funding that will eventually be replaced by permanent capital from equity investors or debt lenders. In Venture Capital, bridge is usually a short-term note (6 to 12 months) that converts to preferred stock (typically the bridge lender

has the right to convert the note to preferred stock at a price that is a 20% to 25% discount from the price of the preferred stock in the next financing round). This type of financing is regularly provided to companies preparing for an IPO with the main goal to improve the capital ratio.

6. Recapitalization / turnaround capital: financing provided to a company at a time of operational or financial difficulty with the intention of improving the company's performance.

1.3.1.3 Venture Capital Financing Rounds

Financing rounds (also called *financing series*) are defined as equity investments, which are performed by one or several VC investors, and which provide additional funding to a venture as it grows. They occur typically every year or two, and allocate shares among the investors and management team based on an agreed valuation. Shares of the same financing round usually bear similar characteristics, e.g. voting rights, par values, or dividend yields. Financing rounds are usually named using alphabet letters, as follows (see TR, 2009, p. 55):

- *Series "A" financing* or *"A" round*: a financing event whereby angel groups or VC investors become involved in a fast growth company that was previously financed by founders and their friends and families. The stock issued in the "A" round of financing is called "series A stock".

- *Series "B" financing* or *"B" round*: a financing event whereby investors such as VC investors and organized angel groups are sufficiently interested in a company to provide additional funds after the "A" round of financing. The stock issued in the "B" round of financing is called "series B stock".

- Subsequent rounds are called "C" round, "D" round, etc. and the stock issued in the respective rounds is called "series C stock", "series D stock", etc.

Moreover, depending on the direction of the valuation change between two consecutive rounds, financing rounds are characterized as "up round", "down round", or "flat round":

- *Down round*: a round of financing whereby the valuation of the company is *lower* than the valuation determined by investors in the precedent round.

- *Up round*: a round of financing whereby the valuation of the company is *higher* than the valuation determined by investors in the precedent round.

- *Flat round* or *even round*: a round of financing whereby the valuation of the company is *unchanged* as compared to the valuation at the precedent round.

1.3.1.4 Venture Capital Exit Events

The *exit* is the liquidation of holdings in a portfolio company by the VC fund. The most frequent methods of exiting an investment are listed in the following:

- *Initial Public Offering*: the sale of common stock to the general investing public for the first time.
- *Merger & Acquisition*: a merger or consolidation, or acquisition by a strategic buyer.
- *Secondary Sale*: the sale of a VC fund's holdings in a portfolio company to other financial investors.
- *Redemption*: the repayment of preference shares or loans subsequently to the exercise of contractual "redemption" rights.
- *Liquidation*: the sale of all or substantially all of the company's assets prior to cessation of operations.

1.3.2 Venture Capital Contracting Terms

1.3.2.1 Incorporation Documents

These documents are drawn up at the time of incorporation of a company, but may be amended within the scope of VC financings. The main incorporation documents include the following:

- *Certificate of Incorporation* (or *Articles of Incorporation* or *Statutes* or *Charter*): A document, filed with a U.S. state by a corporation's founders, describing the purpose, place of business, and other details of a corporation.

- *Bylaws*: The official rules and regulations, which govern a corporation's management.

1.3.2.2 Venture Capital Investment Contracts

The term *VC Investment Contract* stands for a number of different legal agreements of formal nature, which are listed and explained below.

- *Term Sheet* or *Letter of Intent*: a document confirming the intent of an investor to participate in a financing round and summarizing the financial and legal terms of the contemplated transaction. It is usually drafted by the lead investor on behalf of the group of investors who wish to participate in the round. By signing this document, the subject company agrees to begin the legal and due diligence process prior to the closing of the transaction.[5] Although the Term Sheet is not a legally binding document, it reflects an agreement between the parties to proceed to the transaction subject to the incorporated terms, and its essence is usually preserved until the closing of the financing (see TR, 2009, p. 68; Wilmerding, 2006, pp. 9-12).

5 The closing is the conclusion of a financing round whereby all necessary legal documents are signed and capital has been transferred.

- *Amended and Restated Certificate of Incorporation*: the initial Certificate of Incorporation of the company is generally amended and restated within the scope of a VC financing, to establish the rights, preferences, privileges and restrictions of each class and series of the Corporation's stock. It represents a public document, filed with the Secretary of State.

- *Stock Purchase Agreement*: sets forth the basic terms of the purchase and sale of the preferred stock to the investors (such as the purchase price, closing date, conditions to closing) and identifies the other financing documents. Generally it does not set forth either (a) the characteristics of the stock being sold (which are defined in the Certificate of Incorporation) or (b) the relationship among the parties after the closing, such as registration rights, rights of first refusal and co-sale, voting arrangements (these matters often implicate other persons than just the company and the investors in this round of financing, and are usually embodied in separate agreements to which those others persons are parties, or in some cases by the Certificate of Incorporation). The main items of negotiation in the Stock Purchase Agreement are therefore the price and number of shares being sold, and the representations and warranties that the company, and sometimes the Founders as well, must make to the investors.

- *Investors' Rights Agreement*: may cover many different subjects, notably information rights, registration rights, contractual "rights of first offer" or "preemptive rights" (that is rights to purchase securities in subsequent equity financings conducted by the company), and various post-closing covenants.

- *Right of First Refusal and Co-Sale Agreement*: sets forth the rights and obligations of the contracting parties in situations where an existing shareholder wishes to sell his stock to entities outside the company.

- *Management Rights Letter*: specifies the management rights required by the VC investor as part of the agreement to invest in a company. The latter include the right to consult with management on key operational issues, attend board meetings and review information about the company's financial situation.

- *Voting Agreement*: binds shareholders to vote their shares in favor of certain pre-defined matters. When a shareholder refuses to vote as agreed, courts specifically enforce the agreement.

1.3.2.3 Parties of Venture Capital Transactions

The participants in VC transactions are usually identified using the following terms:

- *Portfolio company*: the corporation that has received an investment from a VC firm.
- *Founder(s)*: the individual(s) who founded the portfolio company.
- *Investor(s)*: the VC firm(s) that invested in a portfolio company.
  - *Syndicate*: the group of investors participating in a round of funding.
  - *Lead investor*: typically the VC investor that makes the largest investment in a financing round and manages the documentation and closing of that round. The lead investor sets the price per share of the financing round, thereby determining the valuation of the company.
  - *Co-investor(s)*: the VC investor(s) that does (do) not act as lead investor(s).

1.3.2.4 Financial Instruments

Financial instruments are standardized financial contracts traded in the financial markets. They may include contractual provisions that can be used similarly to standalone covenants. The major groups of financial instruments used by VC firms and relevant in the context of this thesis are defined on the following page.

- *Equity capital*: ownership interest in a company.
  - *Common stock* or *common shares* (also called *straight equity* or *junior equity*): securities representing equity ownership in a corporation, providing voting rights (with one vote exercisable per share), and entitling the holder to participate in the company's success through dividends, capital appreciation, or both. In the event of a liquidation, the claims of secured and unsecured creditors, bondholders, and preferred stockholders take precedence over those of common stockholders. Common stock is usually held by company founders, management and employees.
  - *Preferred stock* or *preferred shares*: capital stock, which typically bears more senior rights than common stock, such as decision-making management control, a promised return on investment (in the form of accrued dividends paid before any dividends are paid to common stock holders), or senior priority in receiving proceeds from a sale or liquidation of the company. The main benefit to owning preferred shares is that the investor has a greater claim on the company's assets than common stockholders.
- *Debt capital*: capital which does not represent ownership in the company. Instead, the company borrows money in the form of non-

transferable loans or transferable securities (bonds, notes, mortgages), which is repayable at maturity. In exchange, it pays the creditor a fixed or variable interest, which depends on the credit rating of the debtor. With the exception of subordinated or junior debt, the creditor's repayment takes precedence over the claims of equity holders in liquidation.

- *Mezzanine capital*: hybrid forms of financing that incorporate characteristics of equity and debt capital. Mezzanine instruments typically used in VC financings are listed in the following.
  - *Convertible security*: A security that can be converted into a different security (generally shares of the issuer's common stock) at the option of the holder, the issuer, or both. Typically, convertible securities convert into a specified number of common shares, which is obtained by multiplying the number of convertible securities held before conversion by a fraction with (a) the nominator equal to the initial purchase price (sometimes plus accrued but unpaid interest or dividends) and (b) the denominator equal to the conversion price specified ex-ante and adapted for certain corporate actions over time.
    * *Convertible preferred stock*: preferred stock that gives an owner the right to convert to common stock.
    * *Convertible debt* or *convertible note*: a debt security, which

allows the lender to exchange the debt for common shares in a company at a preset conversion ratio.

- *Option*: a security which gives the holder the right to purchase shares in a company at a pre-determined price. Options are usually used for long term, phased compensation to management and employees.
- *Warrant*: A warrant is a long term option, usually valid for several years or indefinitely. Typically, warrants are issued concurrently with preferred stocks or bonds in order to increase the appeal of the stocks or bonds to potential investors.
- *Combinations of debt and equity*: instruments composed of debt capital in combination with straight or preferred equity capital. Under these instruments, the investor simultaneously holds both financial instruments and is not granted a conversion option.

In VC contracts, a group of shares which bear similar rights is referred to as a *share class*. In the U.S., VC investors typically differentiate between two share classes: common shares and preferred shares. In Europe, this term is also used to denote different groups of common shares.

1.3.2.5 Price Terms of Venture Capital Transactions

Both the Term Sheet and the closing documents contain information on the current valuation of the company as well as its shareholder structure.

This information is typically specified with the following terms:

- *Valuation*: the equity value of a company, which is typically provided both on a *pre-money* and *post-money* basis:
  - *Pre-money valuation*: the equity value of a company *prior* to the current round of financing. It is obtained by multiplying the total number of shares outstanding (including warrants and issued options) prior to the current financing round by the price per share offered in this round.
  - *Post-money valuation*: the equity value of a company *after* the current round of financing. It is obtained by adding the total amount of equity to be raised in the current round to the pre-money valuation.
- *Capitalization table*: a table showing the owners of a company's shares and their ownership percentages as well as the debt holders. It also lists the forms of ownership, such as common stock, preferred stock, or warrants (see TR, 2009, p. 56).
  - *Pre-money capitalization*: summarizes the capital structure of the company *before* the current round of financing.
  - *Post-money capitalization*: summarizes the capital structure of the company *after* the current round of financing.

1.3.3 Option Pricing Terms

A *Derivative Asset* is an asset whose value is a non-proportional function of the stochastic value of another asset. A *Forward* is a derivative asset that *obligates* the holder to buy or sell a designated asset for a designated delivery price at a designated future time. An *Option*, to the contrary, provides the holder with the *right* to buy or sell a designated asset for a designated price at a designated future time.

A *Real Option* is the right, but not the obligation, to undertake some business decision. *Real Option analysis* as a discipline adapts the mathematical techniques developed for financial options to capital budgeting decisions (for Corporate Finance applications) and, more generally, decision making under uncertainty in "real-life" situations. The definitions provided in this section are drawn from the financial options literature, but are used for the pricing of real options embedded in VC contracts.

The types of options mentioned in this thesis include the following:

- *Call Option* (or Forward): the right (or obligation) to *buy* a specified quantity of some underlying asset by paying a specified exercise price, on or before an expiration date.

- *Put Option* (or Forward): the right (or obligation) to *sell* a specified quantity of some underlying asset for a specified exercise price, on or before an expiration date.

- *European option*: a contract allowing the holder to exercise *exclusively* at maturity.
- *American option*: a contract allowing the holder to exercise *at any time* before or at maturity.
- *Bermudan option*: a contract allowing for *intermittent early exercise*, i.e. for exercise only on certain dates or during certain periods.
- *Barrier option*: an option that has a payoff, which is contingent on the underlying asset reaching some specified level before expiry. The critical level is called the "barrier" and there may be more than one barriers.

The parameters used to specify an option contract and formulate the option value process are defined as follows:

- *Premium*: the option value, that is the dependent variable in the option valuation problem, which should be equal to the amount paid for the option contract.
- *Underlying (asset)*: the asset on which the option value depends. The option payoff is defined as some function of the underlying asset at exercise.
- *Strike* or *exercise price*: the amount for which the underlying can be bought (in case of a call option) or sold (in case of a put option).

- *Investment date*: the date of investment.
- *Initial date*: the earliest date on which the option becomes exercisable (it may differ from the investment date).
- *Maturity (date)*: for European options, maturity is *the* date on which the option can be exercised; for American or Bermudan options, it is the *last* exercise date on which the option can be exercised.
- *Expiration (date) or expiry (date)*: the date on which the option ceases to exist or give the holder any rights (it may differ from the maturity date).
- *Long position*: a position involving the *purchase* of an asset.
- *Short position*: a position assumed when traders *sell* shares they do not own (with some constraints on the length of time before they must be bought back).

1.4 Course of the Investigation

The research objective described in Section 1.2 is broken down into three consecutive steps: (1) identify the pricing methodology applicable in the context of VC contract pricing and specify the general model parameters, (2) gradually build the VC contract pricing model by first analyzing groups of similar provisions and then combining the findings into a comprehensive model, and (3) provide an application of the model to standard investment situations in order to obtain numerical estimates of contract values. This translates into the detailed structure described in the following.

Chapter 2 presents the screening and valuation methodology used to derive the option pricing model for VC contracts. Section 2.1 focuses on the choice of terms analyzed in the model and presents the criteria used to classify embedded options. Section 2.2 identifies the specificities of options embedded in VC contracts and derives the choice of Least Squares Monte Carlo simulation as the option pricing methodology that is best adapted to this context. Section 2.3 specifies the parameters of the pricing model based on time series data of the U.S. Venture Capital industry.

In Chapter 3, the author derives the theoretical model for the pricing of full VC contracts. This analysis is organized around three different groups of provisions, which influence different types of option pricing parameters. More specifically, Section 3.1 analyzes terms that define the payoff func-

tions of embedded options. Section 3.2 focuses on terms that impact the number of shares held by investors. Section 3.3 covers terms that introduce American-type exercise flexibilities. For each group of provisions, the author shows how embedded options can be priced in interaction using Least Squares Monte Carlo Simulation. Finally, Section 3.4 integrates the findings on all three groups of provisions and expands the model to multiple rounds (with several investors and several series of preferred stock).
Chapter 4 provides an application of the pricing model to realistic investment situations. In Section 4.1, the author specifies the price and non-price terms used for the calculations. In Section 4.2, she uses these terms to define three alternative "base" scenarios, which reflect different levels of investor protection. In Section 4.3, she presents the results of the Least Squares Monte Carlo simulation and interprets the results for the different base scenarios.
The conclusion of the thesis is presented in Chapter 5. More specifically, Section 5.1 summarizes the main findings and lists the research contributions. Section 5.2 proposes directions for future research.

2 General Methodology

This chapter describes the methodology employed to identify the options embedded in VC contracts (in Section 2.1), to assess their value while accounting for interaction effects (in Section 2.2), and to specify the parameters of the pricing model (in Section 2.3).

2.1 Screening Methodology

2.1.1 Scope of Analysis

The analysis performed in this thesis addresses deal terms that are representative of current VC structuring practices and industry norms. More specifically, the author focuses on the U.S. market, which represents the largest and oldest VC market worldwide. The analysis is applied to terms, which generate option value (or impact option values generated by other terms) and which are subject to negotiations among the contracting parties. For terms which do not fulfill these requirements, real option analysis would not be applicable or would not provide relevant insights for VC contract design.

To identify the types of options embedded in the relevant terms, the author relies on a standard classification scheme for exotic financial options (see Wilmott, 2006, pp. 368-375), which is based on the following criteria:

- *Time dependence:* do the contract details vary with time?
- *Path dependence (weak or strong):* do option payoffs depend on the path taken by the underlying assets?
- *Dimensionality:* how many underlying independent variables does the option have?
- *Decision flexibility:* does the holder have to make decisions during the life of the contract?
- *Cashflow:* does money change hands during the life of the contract?

Additionally, the analysis accounts for two criteria drawn from the real option literature (see Gamba, 2003; Trigeorgis, 1996), which also apply to options embedded in VC contracts:

- *Ownership:* is the option *proprietary* or *shared* between multiple parties?
- *Interaction:* in the presence of multiple options, are these options *independent* (and hence additive), *mutually exclusive* (if the exercise of one option precludes the exercise of another option) or *compound* (or of "higher order", if the payoff of one option depends on the value of another option)?

These criteria are further explained where they become relevant for the analysis of individual options and interactions in Chapter 3.

2.1.2 Model Legal Documents

To identify relevant terms, the author relies on model VC financing documents published by the NVCA (the trade association representing the U.S. Venture Capital industry). These documents (hereafter the "NVCA model documents") are intended to reflect current customs as well as industry best practice. They include alternative specifications of terms and extensive commentaries, which facilitate the identification of embedded options and their interactions and help to establish distinctions between the formal specification of provisions in the contract and the effective use of these provisions in practice. Notably, certain rights are directly "enforceable", whereas others are used indirectly to increase the bargaining power of investors regarding major corporate decisions. The model documents occasionally diverge from current customs if necessary to avoid internal inconsistencies or redundancies. The initial model documents were the result of a consensus process among the members of the NVCA Model Document Working Group, which consists of leading VC lawyers and VC firms. Since the first publication, they have been regularly revised to reflect legal developments or actual experience. The model documents referred to in this thesis are listed on the following page.

- Term Sheet (hereafter "NVCA Term Sheet"),
- Certificate of Incorporation (amended and restated, hereafter "NVCA Certificate of Incorporation (standard)") and Certificate of Incorporation with Pay-to-Play "Lite" (amended and restated, hereafter "NVCA Certificate of Incorporation (with Pay-to-Play lite)"),
- Investors' Rights Agreement (hereafter "NVCA Investors' Rights Agreement"),
- Voting Agreement (hereafter "NVCA Voting Agreement"),
- Series A Preferred Stock Purchase Agreement (hereafter "NVCA Stock Purchase Agreement"),
- Management Rights Letter (hereafter "NVCA Management Rights Letter"),
- Right of First Refusal and Co-Sale Agreement (amended and restated, hereafter "NVCA Right of First Refusal and Co-Sale Agreement").

These documents were published in May 2010 after the third round of review, comment and revision by the NVCA working group (see NVCA, 2010).

2.1.3 Explanatory Comments

As mentioned in Section 1.2, the regional focus on the U.S. market should not reduce the degree of generality of the option pricing model derived in this thesis. Therefore, throughout the analysis of U.S. terms, the author draws parallels to contracting practices in Europe and derives implications for the pricing of embedded options. These parallels are provided in the form of explanatory comments and derived from an expert interview with Mr. Hassan Sohbi, Partner at the law firm Taylor Wessing LLP in Frankfurt. This approach helps to demonstrate the general applicability of the pricing model while limiting the scope of analysis. Furthermore, it provides guidelines for future scientific research on the economic value of VC contracts in non-U.S. countries.

2.2 Valuation Methodology

2.2.1 Specificities of Options Embedded in Venture Capital Contracts

VC contracts provide investors with claims on the shareholders' equity of the companies in which they invest. The key provisions of these contracts are "contingent clauses", which become exercisable upon the occurrence of specific events such as share issues, share transfers and exit transactions.[1] Since VC portfolio companies are typically not listed, their valuation is not continuously observable. In fact, the only objective (market-defined) estimates of company valuation are produced in the context of new financing rounds and of the exit transaction. These pricing points reflect a consensus among the shareholders and approximate the fair value of the company, assuming that overpricing is precluded by the bargaining power of new investors or buyers, while underpricing is prevented by the fiduciary duties of the Board of Directors and by contractual protective provisions held by VC investors.[2]

To account for the discontinuous adjustment of equity value and for the contingent nature of clauses, the author choses to model the path followed by the equity value not as a continuous diffusion process, but as a jump process that allows for random changes in value upon the occurrence of follow-on VC financing rounds and the exit event (hereafter collectively defined as "Pricing Events").[3]

Over time, VC contracts end up including multiple VC investors with different series of preferred shares and different contractual rights. As a result, contract values for various investors in the same company can

---

[1] The frequency of contingent clauses in the NVCA model documents is documented by the repeated use of the phrase "in the event of [...]" in the legal language.

[2] The Board of Directors has fiduciary responsibility "for the well being and proper guidance of the corporation" (TR, 2009, p. 55), while protective provisions grant VC investors veto rights on issuances of new shares as well as exit transactions (see NVCA Certificate of Incorporation (standard), pp. 13-15; NVCA Term Sheet, pp. 3-4).

[3] A similar approach is taken by Willner (1995) for the valuation of start-up ventures and in Pennings & Lint (1998) for the valuation of R&D projects.

differ significantly. The pricing model developed in this thesis calculates contract values from the perspective of the investor who participated in the first VC financing round. At the same time, it accounts for the fact that certain contractual rights can be jointly held by multiple investors, in which case the options embedded in these rights are shared among multiple parties.

Options embedded in VC contracts can be modeled using two independent variables: *time* (t_i) and *price per share* (or share value) $(P(t_i))$. The variable t_i defines the discrete time steps of the value process (reflecting the occurrence of Pricing Events). The variable $P(t_i)$ is the underlying asset (subject to stochastic jumps upon the occurrence of Pricing Events) and the principal source of randomness affecting embedded options values. These options are either of European or American (respectively Bermudan) type, depending on whether or not the option holders have control over the timing of exit. Contingent clauses may become exercisable upon the same event or upon mutually exclusive events, and the exercise of certain rights may preclude the exercise of others (generating mutually exclusive options). Therefore, as highlighted in Cossin et al. (2002), VC contracts must be interpreted as real option baskets which account for interactions between embedded options.

2.2.2 Derivation of Risk-Neutrality

In the presence of stochastic jumps, markets are incomplete and one cannot construct a riskless hedge portfolio to substantiate the use of risk-neutral valuation (see Merton, 1976). However, the author assumes that the stochastic jumps in the share value of VC-funded companies between consecutive Pricing Events are uncorrelated with the market portfolio, and that VC investors are well diversified at the level of their portfolios. A similar line of argumentation is developed in Willner (1995), who assumes that the jumps in the value of start-up companies reflect new discoveries which are not correlated with the market portfolio. Under this assumption, the jump components generate only non-systematic risk which is fully diversifiable, while the systematic risk is zero. As argued in Merton (1976), risk-neutrality can then be derived based on the Capital Asset Market Model, according to which the expected return of an asset with fully diversifiable non-systematic risk and zero systematic risk simply equals the risk-free rate. This assumption makes risk-neutral valuation applicable in the context of a pricing model with stochastic jumps.

2.2.3 Choice of the Option Pricing Technique

Due to the specificities of options embedded in VC contracts presented in Section 2.2.1, the author choses to use Monte Carlo simulation. This technique was first applied to option pricing by Boyle (1977) and is based on the general derivative pricing paradigm (see Black and Scholes, 1973;

Cox, Ingersoll and Ross, 1985; Harrison and Kreps, 1979; Harrison and Pliska, 1981; Heath, Jarrow and Morton, 1992; Merton, 1973). More specifically, it relies on the fact that the distribution of the terminal underlying values is determined by the process generating future movements of the underlying, and invokes the risk-neutrality assumption to derive the option value. Monte Carlo simulation accommodates complex distributions of the underlying process (including stochastic jumps) as well as exotic option features such as path-dependencies and uncertain parameter values.

To capture American-type exercise flexibilities, the author relies on Least Squares Monte Carlo simulation (LSM) developed by Longstaff and Schwartz (2001). This method combines the (standard) forward simulation of share price paths from investment date to maturity with an assessment (at each time step from the latest possible exercise date to the earliest possible exercise date) of the benefit of exercising versus holding, using a simple regression across stock prices. The effectiveness of LSM for American option pricing problems is widely recognized in the real option literature, and the technique is notably used to derive the option value of internet companies (see Schwartz and Moon, 2000). Furthermore, the LSM method has been extended in Gamba (2003) to cope with interaction effects arising in the presence of multiple options. This extension makes LSM applicable to the mutually exclusive options generated by convertible preferred equity in VC contracts.

The LSM method provides a numerical estimate of *net option value* for a designated *full contract*, covering all provisions of this contract with interactions. For the given contract (in the following called the "base scenario" of the analysis), the option values of *individual terms* can be derived using "adjusted scenarios", which differ from the base scenario only with regard to the individual term under analysis. Hence, the individual term value is obtained by comparing (1) the option value of the *adjusted* scenario (built for the term under analysis) with (2) the option value of the *base* scenario. Hence, the individual term value reflects the change in full contract value inferred by adding this term to the base scenario, respectively by eliminating it from the base scenario. The pricing of a full contract and of n individual terms of this contract therefore requires the setup of $n+1$ scenarios (1 base scenario plus n adjusted scenarios). To compare alternative specifications of a provision (such as Liquidation Preference with *full participation* versus *capped participation*), the base contract and adjusted contracts are chosen accordingly (for example, the base contract would provide for *capped* participation, while the adjusted contract would provide for *full* participation).

The LSM method furthermore allows for an indirect assessment of economic contract value based on the VC investor's expected share of exit proceeds (also called "effective ownership percentage"). In general, the larger the deviation between the VC's share of exit proceeds and his ownership share at the time of investment (or "nominal ownership percentage"), the stronger the value impact of legal terms.

For comparison of two or more alternative configurations of a system (respectively for the comparison of alternative contract scenarios as described above), the best suited variance reduction method is the Common Random Numbers technique (CRN). This technique requires synchronization of random numbers across all configurations, whereby a specific random number used for a specific purpose in one configuration must be used for exactly the same purpose in all other configurations (see Hammersley and Handscomb, 1964; Kahn and Marshall, 1953).

The notation used in the remainder of this thesis closely follows the notations presented in Longstaff and Schwartz (2001) as well as Gamba (2003). To ensure consistency between the notations used for different types of options, European-type claims are treated as special cases of American or Bermudan claims.

2.3 Model Specification

2.3.1 Data Sources

In alignment with the research objective, the parameters of the option pricing model are derived from time series data on VC transactions performed in the U.S.. More specifically, the author relies on a proprietary dataset of the law firm Fenwick & West LLP, which provides the basis for the firm's quarterly report on "Trends in Terms of Venture Financings in Silicon Val-

ley". Additionally, she uses findings from the NVCA Yearbook (see TR, 2009) and from published empirical studies on VC contract design.
The Fenwick & West dataset represents aggregated data from Venture-Source (from Dow Jones) and ThomsonONE (from Thomson Reuters) as well as publicly available sources, which have been reviewed by senior lawyers to ensure that both the financings and the individual terms are classified and interpreted consistently across all observations and over time. The data used by the author covers the main terms of VC financings in the San Francisco Bay Area over the period 2004 to 2008. The sample size of 2,168 financings represents nearly 40% of the total VC financings reported in the region over this period (see NVCA, 2009, p. 27). The findings from this dataset are used to specify the parameters of the underlying asset path (in this section) and to obtain frequencies of use for individual provisions (used in later sections). To ensure the correct interpretation of results, the author has performed an expert interview with Michael Patrick, Partner at the Corporate Group of Fenwick & West in Mountain View and co-author of the deal terms report.

2.3.2 Underlying Asset Path

As described in Section 2.2.1, the underlying asset used for the pricing model is the share value of the portfolio company, which is adjusted discontinuously upon the occurrence of Pricing Events. VC investors seek to exit their investment within a given time frame which is agreed upon by the parties at the time of contracting and typically ranges between three and eight years, depending notably on the stage of development of the portfolio company and the remaining lifetime of the VC fund. The author defines the maximum investment period as the interval $[t_0, t_{max}]$ between the series A investment date (t_0) and the date agreed among the parties (at t_0) as the latest possible exit date (t_{max}). Over this time horizon, there are a random number of Pricing Events and of corresponding jumps in the share price. It is assumed that the direction and magnitude of these jumps are both random. Since adjustments in share value take place exclusively at Pricing Events, the share price remains constant between consecutive jumps.

The path followed by the share price is therefore described as a compound Poisson process, that is as a jump process with zero drift, exponentially distributed waiting times and stochastic jump amplitude:

$$dP(t) = P(t)dN$$

where dN equals 0 with probability $1 - \lambda dt$ and a jump size of J_i with probability λdt.[4]

The waiting time between consecutive jumps is assumed to be exponentially distributed with scale parameter θ.[5] The number of jumps (per time

[4] Baldwin (1979) and Pennings & Lint (1997) use similar jump processes, with stochastic jumps and deterministic (though non-zero) drift rate.

[5] The exponential distribution is mainly chosen for its no-memory property, implying that the probability of arrival of new strategic information does not depend on the

step) follows a homogeneous Poisson process with intensity parameter $\lambda = 1/\theta$. The expected number of price adjustments over the maximum investment period $[t_0, t_{max}]$ is then equal to $\lambda(t_{max} - t_0)$. Empirical findings by Ewens (2009) show that the mean "round-to-round holding period" (i.e. the waiting time between consecutive Pricing Events) equals 1.5 years (in the U.S.). Therefore, the author sets $\theta = 1.5$ (and accordingly $\lambda = 0.67$). The total number of information arrivals over the maximum investment period equals $N = \lambda(t_{max} - t_0) = 0.67 * (t_{max} - t_0)$ with $t_{max} \in [3, 8]$. The date of the last stochastic price jump before t_{max} is defined as follows: $t_N = sup\{t_i : t_i \leq t_{max}\}$.

The amplitude of the jump model is derived from the Fenwick & West LLP dataset, which provides, for each sample financing, the direction of the change in the price per share as compared to the previous round (which allows for distinction between "up rounds" vs. "even rounds" vs. "down rounds"), as well as the magnitude of the price change (expressed as a percentage of the price per share at the previous round).

The statistics on types of rounds can be used to derive the probability distribution of the jump direction, X_i, in the model:

$$X_i = \begin{cases} 1 & \text{with probability } p^u = 66.74\% \text{ (for up rounds);} \\ -1 & \text{with probability } p^d = 21.62\% \text{ (for down rounds);} \\ 0 & \text{with probability } p^e = 11.64\% \text{ (for even rounds).} \end{cases}$$

arrival of past strategic information.

Hence, the probability of positive price jumps amounts to approx. 67%, compared to 22% for down rounds and only 12% for flat rounds.

Similarly, the statistics on the size of changes in the price per share can be used to specify the jump amplitudes for the different types of jumps:

$E(x^u) = 85.82\%$ (average magnitude of upward jumps);

$E(x^d) = 50.10\%$ (average magnitude of downward jumps);

$E(x^e) = 0\%$ (average magnitude of even rounds, by definition).

These results show that that the magnitude of positive jumps is higher than the magnitude of negative jumps. Moreover, as illustrated in Figures 1 and 2, the observed probability distributions of upward versus downward jump magnitudes follow different patterns.

The differences between the two distributions can be explained by the fact that downward jumps cannot exceed 100%, since shareholders have limited liability; in addition, they reflect lower degrees of competition and higher bargaining power of investors in down rounds as compared to up rounds.[6] It is therefore assumed that a better fit to the data can be achieved by modelling the magnitudes of upward versus downward jumps using distinct distributions. Hence, the author performs separate goodness-of-fit tests to estimate the probability distribution function (pdf) providing the best approximation to the observed data in each case.[7]

6 As explained by Michael Patrick (Fenwick & West).

7 A similar argument in favour of asymmetric jump models with mixed distributions has been used for listed stocks, on the basis that prices respond differently to the

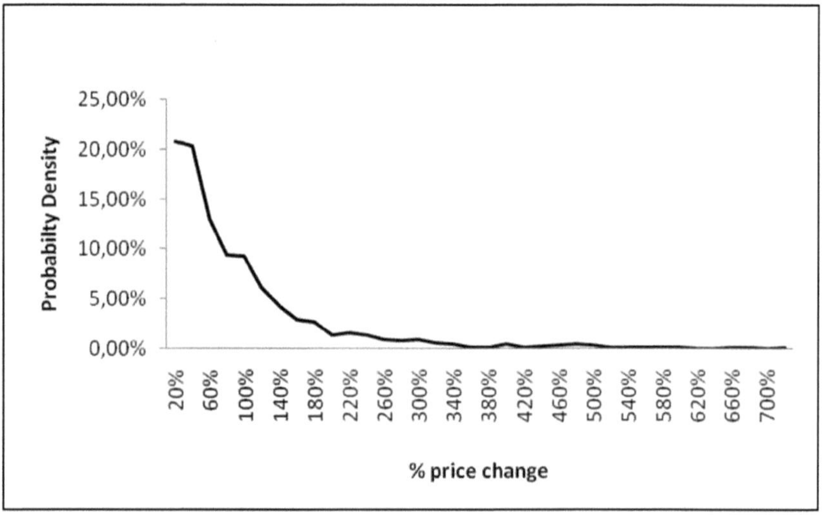

Figure 1: Observed magnitude of upward price changes

Figure 2: Observed magnitude of downward price changes

Figure 1 indicates that the pdf for the magnitude of upward rounds resembles a Weibull distribution with shape parameter $k = 1$ and scale parameter γ (which is equivalent to the exponential distribution).[8] This translates into the following null hypothesis for the magnitude of upward jumps:

$$H_0 : Y_{x^u} \sim Wei(\gamma, 1)$$

The γ parameter of the Weibull distribution is estimated using maximum likelihood estimation. With k = 1, the maximum likelihood estimator for γ is obtained as follows[9]:

$$\hat{\gamma} = \sum_{1}^{n} x_i/n = 0.8582$$

with n being the number of sample rounds.

A chi-squared goodness-of-fit test is then used to test H_0. As shown in Appendix A.1, H_0 cannot be rejected at the $\alpha = 0.10$ level of significance and hence the exponential distribution (or Weibull distribution with $k = 1$) fits the magnitude of upward jumps.

A similar test is performed for the amplitudes of downward jumps. The distribution of observed jump sizes (see Figure 2) shows resemblance to a

arrival of good news and bad news (see Dupoyet, 2004; Ramezani & Zeng, 1998).

8 The author has chosen to use the Weibull distribution for testing purposes, as this allows to assess the fit against a broader range of distributions based on different choices of the shape parameter. The analysis in this chapter is restricted to the Weibull distribution with $k = 1$, which provided the best test results.

9 See Cohen (1965).

uniform distribution, which leads to the following null hypothesis:

$$H_0 : Y_{x^d} \sim U(n)$$

As shown in Appendix A.2, H_0 cannot be rejected at the $\alpha = 0.10$ level of significance and the uniform distribution fits the magnitude of downward jumps.

Based on the previous findings on jump amplitudes and the number of jumps, the underlying process can be specified as follows:

$$P(t) = P(0) \prod_{i=1}^{N^u(t)} [J_i^u + 1] \prod_{i=1}^{N^d(t)} [J_i^d + 1].$$

Accordingly, the instantaneous return is described as:

$$\frac{dP(t)}{P(t)} = J^u(t)dN^u(t) + J^d(t)dN^d(t)$$

with the parameters defined as follows:

- $J^u(t)$ is the percentage up-jump size conditional on an upward jump, defined as: $J^u(t) = x^u(t)$ with $x^u(t)$ distributed *Weibull*$(\gamma, 1)$;
- $J^d(t)$ is the percentage down-jump size conditional on a downward jump, defined as: $J^d(t) = -x^d(t)$ with $x^d(t)$ distributed *uniform*(a, b);
- $N^u(t)$ and $N^d(t)$ are Poisson up and down jump counters with in-

tensities λ^u and λ^d, where

$\lambda^u = \lambda * p^u = 0.67 * 0.67 = 0.45$ and

$\lambda^d = \lambda * p^d = 0.67 * 0.22 = 0.15.$

The Weibull and uniform density functions for the up-jump and down-jump magnitudes are assumed to follow:

- $Y_{x^u}(x^u) = \frac{1}{\gamma} \exp^{-\frac{x^u}{\gamma}}$
  with $x^u \geq 0$, $\gamma = 0.8582$, $E(x^u) = \gamma$ and $\sigma^2_{x^u} = \gamma^2 = 0.7365$;
- $Y_{x^d}(x^d) = \frac{1}{b-a}$
  with $x^d \in [0, 1]$, $E(x^d) = 0.5$ and $\sigma^2_{x^d} = 0.0833$.

As mentioned earlier, the options embedded in VC contracts can be priced as if the expected growth rate for the underlying asset was the risk-free rate, r. Hence, the physical jump model derived above is transformed into a (market diversified) risk-neutral process, by means of the following adjustment (see Dupoyet, 2004; Kou, 2002; Kou and Wang, 2001; Ramezani and Zeng, 1998):

$$\frac{d(P(t))}{P(t)}$$
$$= [r + \lambda(-p^u E(x^u) + p^d E(x^d))]dt + J^u(t)dN^u(t) + J^d(t)dN^d(t)$$
$$= 0.03 - (0.45 * 0.86) + (0.15 * 0.50) + J^u(t)dN^u(t) + J^d(t)dN^d(t)$$
$$= -0.28 + J^u(t)dN^u(t) + J^d(t)dN^d(t)$$

where r is set equal to the Treasury-bill rate averaged over the period 2004 to 2008 (3.05%). All other parameters remain unchanged from above.

2.3.3 Value Process of Embedded Options

This section derives the general value process for all options held by the series A investor (hereafter referred to as "VC_1"), who is assumed to be the only participant in the series A financing.

Let there be one state variable $P(t_i)$, which represents the share value of the portfolio company, and which affects the value of the embedded option (from the perspective of VC_1). Consider the probability space $(\Omega, \mathcal{F}, P)$, where Ω is the state space of all possible paths ω_p of the state variables relevant for pricing the option, $\mathcal{F}$ is the sigma field of disjoint events at time T, and $\mathcal{P}$ is the probability measure corresponding to $\mathcal{F}$. Let the maturity of the option be defined as $T \in [0, t_{max}]$ and the date of the last jump in share value before maturity be $t_M = sup\{t_i : t_i \leq T\}$. Let there be M discrete stopping times, $t_0 \leq t_1 \leq t_2 \leq \cdots \leq t_M$, with $t_0 = 0$.[10]

The payoff $\Pi(\omega, t_k; t, t_M)$ is defined as the cash flow deriving from the option for VC_1 at time t_k (representing the investor's proceeds from the exit transaction), and $I_{vc_1}(\omega, t_k; t, t_M)$ is defined as the cumulated amount invested by VC_1 at time t_k, when the state path ω_p is realized, given that the option is not terminated at or before time t, and that the investor follows the optimal exercise strategy for all exercise dates t_k between time t and t_M, with $t < t_k \leq t_M$. K defines the exercise restrictions in the form of sets of time in which exercise of the option is allowed. These sets of

[10] These stopping times do not have to be equivalent to the time steps used for the simulation model.

time must concur with the time steps used for the simulation of the jump process (see Section 2.3.2). Note that the presence of a barrier condition may cause K to differ across paths because the option might become exercisable only in certain paths due to the evolution of the state variables in these paths. Let the value of the claim at t be $F(t, P(t))$.

If the contingent claim can be exercised exclusively at the last time step before maturity, t_M, it is a European-type claim. The value of this claim at any time t equals:

$$F(t, P_t) = \frac{1}{n}\sum_{p=1}^{n} e^{-r(t_M - t)} E_t^*[\Pi(\omega_p; t_M, P_{t_M}) - I_{vc_1}(\omega_p; t_M, P_{t_M})]$$

where $E_t^*[\cdot]$ is the expected value in a risk-neutral world, conditional on the information available at t, and n is the number of simulation paths.

If the contingent claim can be exercised at any time before t_M, it is an American-type claim; respectively, if exercise is restricted to certain dates in $[t_1, t_M]$, it is a Bermudan-type claim. In these cases, the value of the claim at any time t equals:

$$F(t, P_t) = \frac{1}{n}\sum_{p=1}^{n} \max_{t_k \in K_p}\{e^{-r(t_k - t)} E_t^*[\Pi(\omega_p; t_k, P_{t_k}) - I_{vc_1}(\omega_p; t_k, P_{t_k})]\}$$

where $K_p(\omega_p; t, t_M)$ is the set of possible exercise dates in $[t, t_M]$ for simulation path ω_p with regards to $\{\mathcal{F}_t\}$.

2.3.4 Dependent Variables

To derive the contract pricing model in Chapter 3, the author relies on a set of additional dependent variables, which are influenced by the independent variables of the model as well as by certain contractual provisions. These variables are defined in the following.

N^c_{tot}	total number of shares (fully diluted)
$N^p_{vc_1}$	number of preferred shares held by VC_1
$N^c_{vc_1}$	number of common shares receivable by VC_1 upon conversion
N^p_{VC}	number of preferred shares held by all VC investors
N^c_{VC}	number of common shares receivable by all VC investors (upon conversion of their preferred shares)
I_{VC}	total amount invested by all preferred holders
V_{pre}	pre-money valuation of the company (fully diluted)
V_{post}	post-money valuation of the company (fully diluted)
α	ownership percentage of VC_1 (fully diluted)
β	ownership percentage of all preferred holders (fully diluted)
C_{vc_1}	conversion price applicable to preferred shares held by VC_1

Variables defined on a "fully diluted" basis rely on the number of common shares *outstanding* and *deemed outstanding* after conversion of all convertible securities and after exercise of all stock options.

2.3.5 Trigger Events

As explained in Section 2.2.1, the key provisions of VC contracts become exercisable upon occurrence of specific events which represent the "trigger events" of embedded options. Since these events influence the exercise restrictions of embedded options, they must be specified before analyzing contract provisions and deriving the contract pricing model in Chapter 3. Hereby, the author makes a distinction between Pricing Events and Share Transfers.

2.3.5.1 Pricing Events

Pricing Events reflect objective pricing points of the company and generate the stochastic jumps in the underlying process (see Sections 2.2.1 and 2.3.2). They include *share issues* and *exit transactions*.
Share issues are formally defined in the NVCA model documents as "issuances of additional equity securities, whether or not authorized, as well as rights, options, or warrants to purchase such equity securities, or securities of any type whatsoever that are, or may become, convertible or exchangeable into or exercisable for such equity securities" (NVCA Investors' Rights Agreement, p. 4). In most cases, these events represent follow-on VC financings via issuances of convertible preferred shares. To limit the complexity of the model, future share issues will therefore be interpreted as "issuances of additional convertible preferred equity securities to VC investors" (hereafter called follow-on VC Financings).

The offer size of any follow-on VC financing is assumed to be a fixed percentage of the company's valuation at that round. Let η be the percentage obtained by dividing the amount raised in any follow-on round i (with $i > 0$) by the post-money valuation at that round. The post-money valuation at round k can then be derived from the total number of shares at the previous round $(i - 1)$ as follows:

$$V_{post}(t_i) = \frac{N_{tot}^{c}(t_{i-1}) * P(t_i)}{(1 - \eta)}$$

Accordingly, the total number of shares (fully-diluted) after this round is:

$$N_{tot}^{c}(t_i) = \frac{N_{tot}^{c}(t_{i-1})}{1 - \eta}$$

The parameter η is estimated using the NVCA Yearbook statistics, by dividing the average investment size of follow-on rounds by the average post-money valuation of follow-on rounds (see TR, 2009, pp. 31, 41-42). Hence, the parameter is specified as $\eta = 15\%$.

The second type of Pricing Event are *exit transactions*, which include the following (mutually exclusive) events:[11]

- *Initial Public Offering (IPO):* a sale of common stock to the general investing public for the first time.

---

[11] See NVCA Certificate of Incorporation (standard), p. 6, pp. 8-9, p. 28.; NVCA Voting Agreement, p. 9.

- *Sale of the Company (CS):* this term covers Stock Sales and Deemed Liquidation Events.
  - *Stock Sale (or sale of control):* a transaction in which a person acquires from stockholders of the company shares representing more than fifty percent of the outstanding voting power.
  - *Deemed Liquidation Event:* a merger or consolidation, or the sale (or other disposition) of all or substantially all the assets of the corporation.
- *Liquidation Event (LE):* voluntary or involuntary dissolution, liquidation or winding up of the corporation.

Generally, IPOs only become attractive at very high levels of company valuation, at which the expected proceeds compensate for the high cost (direct and indirect expenses) and risk (lock-up period and systematic risk) of the transaction. Liquidation Events, to the contrary, are most likely to occur at low levels of valuation, that is when major technology or market uncertainties remain unsolved over time, or when the company runs out of cash.[12] Company Sales, on the other hand, can theoretically be performed at any time, independently of company performance, provided that the company or the majority investor can identify a buyer willing to pay the fair company value.

[12] As confirmed in the expert interview with Hassan Sohbi (Taylor Wessing).

Hence, the uncertain dates of Liquidation (τ_{LE}) and IPO (τ_{IPO}) are modeled as *random times of class 1* (see Karoui and Martellini, 2001, p. 6).

Definition 1 (Class 1 Random Time) *A random (jump) time τ is said to be Class 1 random time if τ is a stopping time of the filtration $\mathbb{F}$ generated by asset prices, that is if the event $t_i < \tau$ is $\mathcal{F}_t$-measurable for all $t_i \geq 0$.*

In this case, observing the asset price up to the i-th jump provides full knowledge about whether τ has occurred or not. Hence, the timing risk is embedded within asset price risk and no new uncertainty is added to the economy. Put differently, the IPO and Liquidation Events are interpreted as *path-dependent* events and the embedded options which are triggered by these events are effectively transformed into *barrier options*. The specification of these path-dependent events requires the definition of barriers (or threshold levels).

For the liquidation threshold, the author makes the following assumption.

Assumption 1 (Liquidation Threshold) *The company goes out of business when the price per share falls below a certain minimum threshold, which is calculated using a percentage discount of $\delta = 75\%$ on the initial share value at t_0. Thus, the date of the Liquidation Event is defined as follows:*

$$\forall t_i > 0 : \tau_{LE} = \begin{cases} \inf\{t_i : P(t_i) \leq h_{LE}\} & \textit{if } \exists t_i / P(t_i) \leq h_{LE} \\ 0 & \textit{if not} \end{cases}$$

with $h_{LE} = P(t_0) * (1 - \delta)$, $\delta = 0.75$.

Hereby, it must be noted that a definition of the liquidation threshold based on the Price Per Share is only justifiable in the absence of structural changes such as stock splits or reverse splits. According to the findings from the Fenwick & West dataset, structural changes occur in less than 7% of all sample financings. Moreover, they generally reflect *formal* rearrangements of the company's capital structure and are not driven by changes in company performance. For those reasons, abstracting from structural changes comes with no major loss of generality and the definition of the liquidation threshold is justified in this context.
For IPOs, the threshold level is derived from median pre-money valuations of VC-backed IPOs in the U.S. for the 10-year period 1999-2008 (see TR, 2009, p. 44).

Assumption 2 (IPO Threshold) *The company goes public when the pre-offer valuation of the company exceeds \$200m. The IPO date is therefore defined as follows:*

$$\forall t_i > 0 : \tau_{IPO} = \begin{cases} \inf\{t_i : V_{pre}(t_i) \geq h_{IPO}\} & \textit{if}\, \exists t_i / V_{pre}(t_i) \geq h_{IPO} \\ 0 & \textit{if not} \end{cases}$$

with $h_{IPO} = \$200m.$

The offer amount of the IPO is set equal to 27% of the post-offer valuation. This percentage is obtained from the NVCA Yearbook statistics by dividing median offer amounts by median post-offer valuations over the period 1999-2008 (see TR, 2009, p. 44). Hence, the post-offer valuation and the total number of shares after IPO are obtained as follows:

$$\begin{aligned} V_{post}(\tau_{IPO}) &= N^c_{tot}(t_{IPO-1}) * P(\tau_{IPO})/(1-0.27) \\ N^c_{tot}(\tau_{IPO}) &= N^c_{tot}(t_{IPO-1})/(1-0.27) \end{aligned}$$

Accounting for the threshold condition above, $V_{post}(\tau_{IPO}) \geq \$274m$, and the offer amount is equal or superior to $\$74m$.

If neither an IPO nor a Liquidation Event have occurred before or at the last time step t_N (i.e. the date of the last jump in share value before t_{max}), it is assumed that a Sale of the Company is initiated by either the company (reflecting a Deemed Liquidation Event) or by the VC investors (reflecting a Stock Sale) at t_N.[13]

Assumption 3 (Sale condition) *The company initiates a Sale if no other exit transaction has occurred until the last jump date t_N. Hence, the date of the Company Sale is defined as follows:*

$$\forall t_i > 0 : \tau_{CS} = \begin{cases} t_N & \textit{if } \tau_{IPO} = \tau_{LE} = 0, \textit{ and} \\ 0 & \textit{otherwise} \end{cases}$$

[13] The author assumes that a trader buyer or merger partner willing to pay fair company value can be found at this date. In reality, the transaction may only be possible with a certain delay or with concessions on the offer price.

By combining the above assumptions, the uncertain date of the exit transaction can be defined as follows:

$$\tau_{exit} = \begin{cases} \tau_{IPO} & \text{if } \tau_{LE} > \tau_{IPO} > 0, \text{ or if } \tau_{IPO} > 0 \wedge \tau_{LE} = 0 \\ \tau_{LE} & \text{if } \tau_{IPO} > \tau_{LE} > 0, \text{ or if } \tau_{LE} > 0 \wedge \tau_{IPO} = 0 \\ \tau_{CS} & \text{if } \tau_{IPO} = \tau_{LE} = 0 \end{cases}$$

with $h_{IPO} = \$200m$ and $h_{LE} = 0.25 * P(t_0)$.

2.3.5.2 Share Transfers

In the NVCA model documents, Share Transfers are called "Proposed Key Holder Transfers" and defined as "any assignment, sale, offer to sell, pledge, mortgage, hypothecation, encumbrance, disposition of or any other like transfer or encumbering of any Transfer Stock (or any interest therein) proposed by any of the Key Holders"[14]. These transfers are initiated by an individual shareholder (or "key holder") in order to reduce his exposure or to fully exit the investment, for reasons which are specific to this shareholder and not related to company performance or to the anticipated exit horizon. For example, Secondary Sales (which are share transfers from an existing VC investor to another financial investor) are generally caused by reasons particular to this investor such as the lifetime of the VC fund or the divestment of a complete portfolio.

Since Share Transfer events are unrelated to jumps in the underlying value,

14 NVCA Right of First Refusal and Co-Sale Agreement, p. 3.

their occurrence has to be modeled as Class 2 random time (see Karoui and Martellini, 2001, p. 7):

Definition 2 (Class 2 Random Time) *A random (jump) time τ is said to be Class 2 random time if τ is a positive random variable, measurable with respect to the sigma algebra $\mathcal{A}$, which is not a stopping time of the filtration $\mathbb{F}$ generated by asset prices, that is if there is a $\tau \geq 0$ such that the event $t_i < \tau$ is not $\mathcal{F}_t$-measurable.*

Hence, observing asset prices up to date t_i does not provide full information on whether τ has occurred or not and the uncertainty over the time horizon induces some form of incompleteness into the pricing model.

Share Transfers trigger the exercise of two key provisions of VC contracts: Rights of First Refusal and Tag-along Rights. The provisions are shared between multiple parties and exercisable in a specific order and over multiple rounds of allocation. An in-depth analysis of these provisions with regard to embedded options is only possible in a game-theoretic setting and based on sequential compound options. Accordingly, covering these provisions would not only require the introduction of a class 2 random time, but also introduce sequential compound option problems in a game-theoretic setting. This would dramatically increase the complexity of the pricing model and likely bias the option values obtained for the remaining provisions. Therefore, the contract pricing model developed in this thesis abstracts from Share Transfer events and does not cover Rights of First Refusal and Tag-Along Rights.

3 Venture Capital Contract Pricing Model

In this chapter, the author identifies the types of options embedded in VC contracts and shows how they can be priced while accounting for interaction effects. To facilitate the analysis, the terms are categorized into three groups, depending on the type of option parameters that they influence. The groups are first analyzed separately (in Sections 3.1 to 3.3) and then integrated into a comprehensive model (in Section 3.4).

3.1 Provisions Defining the Payoff Functions

The most common security used for VC financings in the U.S. is convertible preferred stock. Common stock is only issued exceptionally, for example within the scope of pre-IPO financing rounds, where institutional types of investors would be offered common stock at a discount to existing shares.[1] Convertible preferred provides the VC investor with both

[1] In certain European countries, convertible preferred shares are not a commonly used security; however, the corresponding preferred rights are replicated through contractual obligations defined at the level of shareholder agreements. This was explained

downside protection and upside participation, via Liquidation Preference and (Optional and Mandatory) Conversion Rights. These provisions define the payoff functions of embedded options and are therefore analyzed together in this section. The section also covers Piggyback Registration Rights, since they are tightly linked to Mandatory Conversion Rights.

3.1.1 Mandatory Conversion and Piggyback Registration

Mandatory (or Automatic) Conversion is a "given" in VC contracts.[2] It specifies that convertible preferred stock automatically converts to common stock upon occurrence of certain trigger events, which typically include (a) a Qualified Public Offering (QPO), defined as a public offering that meets certain minimum conditions, or (b) a majority (or sometimes super-majority) vote of the holders of preferred stock.[3] Mandatory Conversion represents a protection mechanism for both the company and the investor. It protects the company by clearing the way towards an IPO in success scenarios (since underwriters typically require that the company has a single class of equity) and by mitigating the investor's incentive to "grandstand" (i.e. to take a company public prematurely in order to im-

by Hassan Sohbi (Taylor Wessing).

2 This is mentioned in the NVCA Yearbook (see TR, 2009, p. 57) and has been confirmed by Michael Patrick (Fenwick & West).

3 Model specifications of the Mandatory Conversion clause are provided in the NVCA Certificate of Incorporation (standard), pp. 30-31, and in the NVCA Term Sheet, p. 5. Formally, conversion can also be forced upon the VC investor if he forgoes to (fully) exercise his Preemption Right; since this scenario represents a special case of "Pay-to-play" provisions, it will be covered in Section 3.2.3. together with these provisions.

prove his reputation).[4] It protects the VC investor, since the company can only perform an IPO if the offering meets certain minimum requirements, or if it obtains the consent of a majority of investors. At the same time, this obligation to convert is costly to the investor, since he loses the rights attached to preferred shares. This cost of conversion is all the higher, the earlier the development stage of the company and the more important the downside protection attached to the preferred shares. For this reason, VC investors would only *voluntarily* agree on foregoing their preferred rights in exceptional situations, for example if the conversion of their preferred shares into common shares allows them to gain voting majority at the Board of Directors (e.g. when the tie-breaking seat is filled by common and preferred holders voting as a single class, on as-converted basis), or if conversion is required by an external investor as a prerequisite for the infusion of new funds. Hence, Automatic Conversion is rarely initiated by consent of the preferred holders, but in most cases triggered by a QPO event. Therefore, the analysis will focus on the trigger event in form of a QPO, which is typically defined using the following criteria:[5]

1. Minimum valuation (pre- or post-money): guarantees the investors a minimum return on investment.

2. Minimum proceeds (gross or net): guarantees that the offering compensates for the high IPO-related expenses.

---

[4] These mechanisms are described in further detail in Camp (2002), Black & Gilson (1998), and Gompers (1996).

[5] See NVCA Certificate of Incorporation (standard), p. 28; Camp (2002).

Sometimes, the QPO conditions also include a minimum public float, a minimum price per share, or both. The minimum public float condition is indirectly covered by the minimum proceeds condition mentioned above.[6] The minimum price per share condition represents a formal requirement, which is not necessarily related to company performance or to the scope and quality of a public offering (since the price per share may also change due to structural changes such as share splits). Therefore, the remainder of this section will abstract from the public float and share price conditions. As determined by the IPO threshold derived in Section 2.3.5, the pre-offer valuation of the company is at least $\$200m$ and the gross proceeds from IPO amount to at least $\$73m$. Since QPO conditions are usually defined at levels that are inferior to these IPO threshold levels, any IPO event in the option pricing model meets the QPO conditions.[7] Accordingly, the date of QPO can be set equal to the date of IPO, τ_{IPO}.

In terms of embedded derivatives, the Mandatory Conversion provision generates a forward contract on common shares, since the VC investor is *obliged* to convert his preferred shares into common shares in the event of an IPO. Upon conversion, the VC investor holds a position of α *long call with* $E = 0$, which represents the value of his common shares (on as-converted basis). Investors, management and employees usually agree

6 Under the assumptions that no shareholder (other than employees) holds less than 10% of total shares outstanding prior to the IPO and that all members of the pre-IPO shareholder base are subject to a lock-up period after IPO, the free float equals the gross proceeds to the company.

7 This was confirmed by Hassan Sohbi (Taylor Wessing).

on a so-called “lock-up period” (i.e. a period of at least 180 days after the IPO, during which they refrain from selling their shares to the public).[8] This avoids large sales of stock immediately after the IPO and allows the company to build interest among potential buyers of its shares. Since VC financings are by definition investments in private companies, it can be assumed that VC investors aim at using the IPO as an exit channel and do not speculate on the future development of the company. Accordingly, they sell their shares as soon as possible after the IPO, that is immediately after expiration of the lock-up period. Thus, the maturity of the forward contract from Mandatory Conversion is defined as follows:

$T_{MC} = \inf\{t_i : t_i \geq \tau_{IPO} + 0,5\}.$

In the U.S., shares in a public company cannot be sold to the public unless they have been registered with the Securities and Exchange Commission (SEC) or are exempt from registration.[9] Hence, Mandatory Conversion is only valuable in the presence of Piggyback Registration Rights, which entitle the VC investor to “piggyback” on any registrations initiated by the company or by other investors.[10] Therefore, VC investors invariably require Piggyback Registration rights as a condition of funding for U.S.-

---

8 The lock-up period is usually defined in a “Market Stand-Off Agreement” (see NVCA Investors’ Rights Agreement, pp. 16-17; NVCA Term Sheet, p. 8).

9 A registration is the process whereby shares of a company are registered with the SEC under the Securities Act of 1933 in preparation for a sale of the shares to the public (see TR, 2009, p. 65).

10 Investors can initiate registrations using their “Demand Registration” rights; these rights influence the exercise restrictions of embedded options and not their payoff functions, and are therefore covered in Section 3.3.2.2.

based companies.[11] Piggyback Registration is not valuable in isolation, since registration is only feasible for common shares. However, if analyzed in interaction, Mandatory Conversion and Piggyback Registration generate a full-fledged forward contract:

Proposition 1 (Automatic Conversion Plus Piggyback Registration) *In the presence of Automatic Conversion and Piggyback Registration, the VC investor is effectively granted a forward contract on registered common shares of the company. The maturity of this contract is T_{MC}.*

This contract allows the VC investor to convert his preferred shares into common shares, register these shares with the SEC, and sell them to the public after expiration of the lock-up period, at market price. Under the assumption that the VC investor exits the investment as soon as possible after IPO, he does not acquire additional shares in or after the IPO. Accordingly, the number of common shares sold after expiration of the lock-up period equals the total number of common shares held at the last financing round before the IPO:

$$N_{vc_1}^{c}(T_{MC}) = N_{vc_1}^{c}(\tau_{IPO}) = N_{vc_1}^{c}(\tau_{IPO-1})$$

---

[11] For investments in non-U.S. companies, VCs do generally not pay major attention to Registration rights at the time of contracting. However, if an IPO in the U.S. evolves as a likely exit scenario for a company over time, VC investors would usually ask for the (a posteriori) inclusion of Registration rights into their contract before voting in favour of an IPO.

Applying the conversion price in effect at the date of IPO, the number of common shares receivable upon conversion is obtained as follows:

$$N^{c}_{vc_1}(\tau_{IPO-1}) = N^{p}_{vc_1}(\tau_{IPO-1}) * \frac{P(t_0)}{C_{vc_1}(\tau_{IPO-1})}$$

The variables $N^{p}_{vc_1}(\tau_{IPO-1})$ and $C_{vc_1}(\tau_{IPO-1})$ are adjusted over time to account for the exercise of Preemption rights, Anti-dilution rights and Pay-to-play penalties. These adjustments are explained in Section 3.2. The payoff function of the forward contract can be written as:

$$\Pi_{MC}(T_{MC}, P(T_{MC})) = N^{c}_{vc_1}(\tau_{IPO-1}) * P(T_{MC})$$

Accordingly, the value of the forward contract at $t \leq T_{MC}$ is:

$$\begin{aligned} &F_{MC}(t, P(t)) \\ &= e^{-r(T_{MC}-t)} E^{*}_{t}[\Pi_{MC}(T_{MC}, P(T_{MC})) - I_{vc_1}(T_{MC}, P(T_{MC}))] \end{aligned}$$

$I_{vc_1}(T_{MC}, P(T_{MC}))$ is defined as the cumulated investment of VC_1.

3.1.2 Liquidation Preference

By definition, convertible preferred stock provides for some type of *Liquidation Preference*, which grants its holders the right to receive a minimum value for their stock in "preference" to the holders of other classes of stock upon occurrence of certain exit events (see TR, 2009, p. 57). As argued by Smith (2005), Liquidation rights almost never confer the VC investor

a contractual right to liquidate the portfolio company. Therefore, they should be understood as *protective* exit rights and not as *initiatory* exit rights. The major function of Liquidation rights is to protect the VC investor against opportunistic liquidation by a controlling entrepreneur and to increase his incentive to force liquidation through exercise of other contractual rights (e.g. via board voting rights) in circumstances when the entrepreneur would like to maintain the status quo. The payment of the liquidation amount is effectively triggered by the occurrence of a Liquidation Event or the Sale of the Company in the form of a Stock Sale or a Deemend Liquidation Event. The trigger event in the form of Stock Sale is not listed in the Charter, since this type of transaction may not be within the control of the corporation. However, the "Restrictions on Sales of Control of the Company" in the Voting Agreement ensure that the preferred holders receive the same share of exit proceeds in the event of a Stock Sale than in the case of a Deemed Liquidation Event.[12]
This leads to the following proposition for embedded derivatives:

Proposition 2 (Liquidation rights) *Liquidation rights can be valued by means of a European option which becomes exercisable upon the occurrence of the earliest of a Liquidation Event or a Sale of the Company, that*

[12] See NVCA Certificate of Incorporation (standard), pp. 6-7; NVCA Voting Agreement, p. 9.

is at

$$T_{LP} = \begin{cases} \tau_{LE} & \textit{if } \tau_{IPO} > \tau_{LE} > 0, \textit{ or if } \tau_{LE} > 0 \wedge \tau_{IPO} = 0; \\ \tau_{CS} & \textit{if } \tau_{IPO} = \tau_{LE} = 0. \end{cases}$$

The payoff function of this claim can be derived from the definition of the "liquidation amount", as well as the degree of "seniority" of the preferred holder. The *liquidation amount* usually contains the following elements:

- a *fixed amount* equalling a multiple of the initial investment (usually 1x to 3x); plus
- (if specified) a *variable amount* conditional on total exit proceeds (also called "participating" feature); plus
- (if specified) *dividends* defined as "cumulative" or "non-cumulative" dividends.

The degree of *seniority* defines the ranking order among the different shareholders with regard to the payout of the liquidation amount. Thus, if preferred shares issued in later rounds rank *senior* to the shares issued in prior rounds, the holders of these shares are entitled to be paid out their liquidation amount before any payments are made on *junior* shares. By definition, seniority only becomes relevant in the presence of multiple financing rounds. In the Fenwick & West dataset, 46% of all sample financings have senior Liquidation Preference.

Dividends payable to preferred holders are usually defined as *cumulative* or *non-cumulative* dividends. Cumulative dividends (also called "accrued") grant the right to receive dividends that have cumulated over time (independently of whether they were declared or not) and which have not been paid out in full prior to the exit event. In the Fenwick & West dataset, less than 6% of all sample financings provide for cumulative dividends. Non-cumulative dividends (also called "declared but unpaid") are payable to owners of preferred stock only if they were declared by the Board of Directors and if the company has sufficient cash available. This type of dividends is rarely employed in VC contracting and not covered in the Fenwick & West database. Given that dividends are infrequently used in the U.S. (and generally represent a minor share of total exit proceeds), these rights will not be covered by the pricing model.

To derive the payoff functions of embedded options in this section, the company is assumed to perform a single financing round with a single investor (VC_1). Under this assumption, no additional preferences are issued after t_0. The assumption will be relaxed in Section 3.4 to derive the comprehensive pricing model, which accounts for all terms in interaction as well as multiple financing rounds with multiple investors and series of preferred stock.

3.1.2.1 No participation

The simplest form of the Liquidation Right is created by *non-participating* preferred stock. The liquidation amount is simply defined as a multiple (m) of the amount invested. Since there is only one round with one investor (by assumption), the total amount invested by VC_1 at exit simply equals his initial investment $I_{vc_1}(t_0) = N^p_{vc_1}(t_0) * P(t_0)$. To simplify the notation, $I_{vc_1}(t_0)$ will be abbreviated as I in the remainder of this chapter. At exit, the VC investor receives either his liquidation amount mI (if total proceeds are equal or superior to the liquidation amount), or the totality of exit proceeds $V(T_{LP}) = N^c_{tot}(T_{LP}) * P(T_{LP})$ (if total proceeds are inferior to the liquidation amount). Hence, the payoff function of non-participating preferred stock can be replicated using the following option basket:

- one long call with $E = 0$;
- one short call with $E = mI$.

Figure 3 shows the payoff diagram for Liquidation Preference without participation.[13] As illustrated, the total payoff from this option basket is:

$$\begin{aligned}\Pi_{LP}(T_{LP}, P(T_{LP})) &= \max\{V(T_{LP}), 0\} - \max\{V(T_{LP}) - mI, 0\} \\ &= V(T_{LP}) - \max\{V(T_{LP}) - mI, 0\} \\ &= \min\{V(T_{LP}), mI\}\end{aligned}$$

[13] A payoff diagram is a graph which plots the value of an option at expiry as a function of the underlying asset.

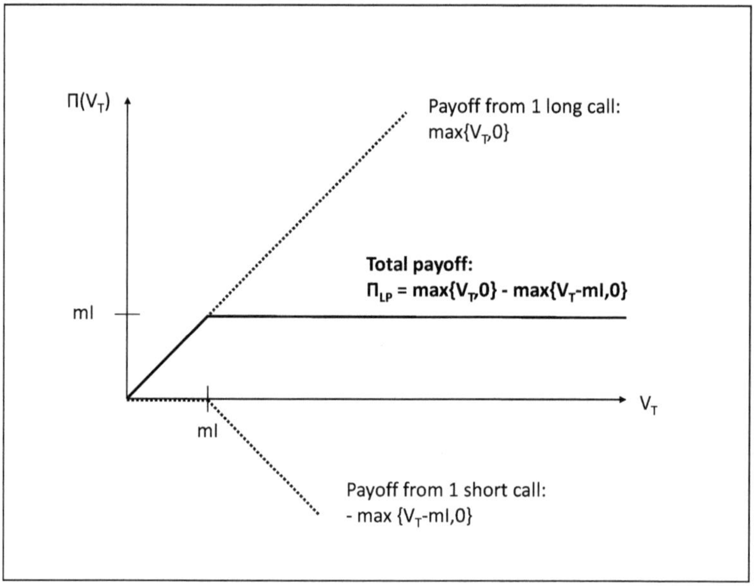

Figure 3: Payoff diagram for no participation

3.1.2.2 Full participation

In the case of *full participation*, the VC investor does not only receive a multiple of his invested amount in preference to the holders of common shares, but also participates in exit values above this multiple on an as-converted basis. The participation feature has major effects on the incentive structures of both parties: while it deters the entrepreneur from favoring mergers over public offerings, it prevents VC investors from strategically vetoing a worthwhile merger proposal in hope for an uncertain public offering (see Smith, 2005, p. 348).

The payoff function with full participation differs from the payoff function without participation for exit proceeds exceeding the Liquidation Preference. At those levels, the payoff to VC_1 equals his pro-rata ownership percentage (fully diluted) at exit, defined as follows:

$$\alpha(T_{LP}) = \frac{N^c_{vc_1}(T_{LP})}{N^c_{tot}(T_{LP})}$$

The simplifying assumption of one single financing round implies that $\alpha(T_{LP}) = \alpha(t_0)$ (hereafter abbreviated as α). The payoff function of preferred shares with full participation can be replicated using the following option basket:

- one long call with $E = 0$.
- $(1 - \alpha)$ short calls with $E = mI$. Hereby, the VC investor participates in exit proceeds above the Liquidation Preference on an

as-converted basis (that is according to the fraction of total equity he would be holding if he converted his preferred shares into common shares).

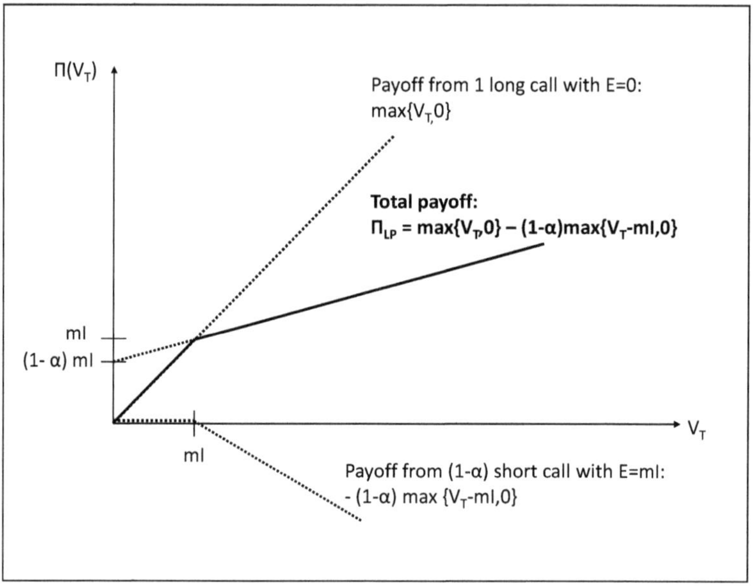

Figure 4: Payoff diagram for full participation

Figure 4 shows the payoff diagram for Liquidation Preference with full participation. The total payoff function for full participation is defined as follows:

$$\begin{aligned}
&\Pi_{LP}(T_{LP}, P(T_{LP})) \\
&= \max\{V(T_{LP}), 0\} - (1-\alpha)\max\{V(T_{LP}) - mI, 0\} \\
&= \min\{V(T_{LP}), mI\} + \alpha \max\{V(T_{LP}) - mI, 0\}
\end{aligned}$$

3.1.2.3 Capped participation

In the presence of *capped participation*, the investor participates only up to a pre-specified cap, c, which is defined as a multiple of the invested amount (typically 3x to 5x).

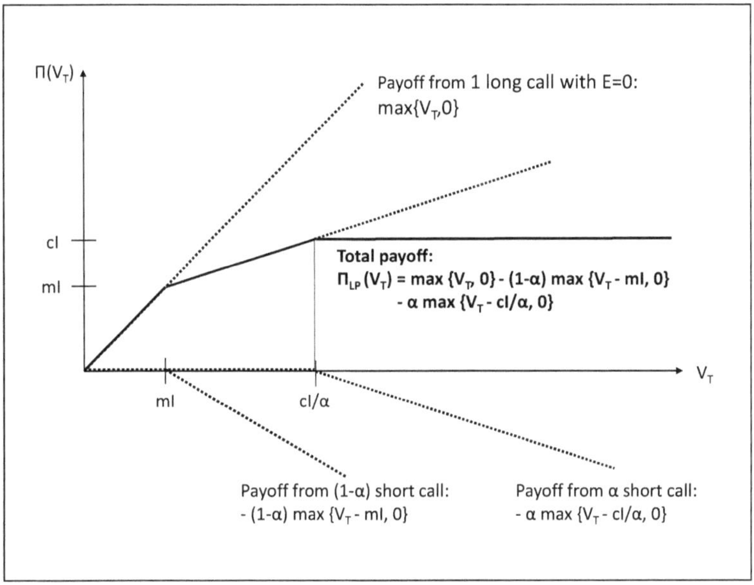

Figure 5: Payoff diagram for capped participation

As shown in Figure 5, capped participation generates the same payoff function as full participation for levels of total exit proceeds below $\frac{cI}{\alpha}$. For exit proceeds above this level, the VC investor's payoff stays cI. Consequently, the total payoff function for capped participation can be represented as a basket of the following options:

- one long call with $E = 0$
- $(1-\alpha)$ short call with $E = mI$
- α *short call with* $E = \frac{cI}{\alpha}$

The total basket yields the following payoff function:

$$
\begin{aligned}
&\Pi_{LP}(T_{LP}, P(T_{LP})) \\
&\quad = \max\{V(T_{LP}), 0\} - (1-\alpha)\max\{V(T_{LP}) - mI, 0\} \\
&\qquad -\alpha \max\{V(T_{LP}) - \frac{cI}{\alpha}, 0\} \\
&\quad = \min\{V(T_{LP}), mI\} + \alpha \max\{V(T_{LP}) - mI, 0\} \\
&\qquad -\alpha \max\{V(T_{LP}) - \frac{cI}{\alpha}, 0\}
\end{aligned}
$$

According to the Fenwick & West dataset, nearly 65% of all sample financings grant the investor participation in proceeds above the Liquidation Preference; in approx. 47% of the cases, this participation is capped. Liquidation multiples (preferences with $m > 1$) are found in 20% of the *senior* sample rounds.[14]

[14] As explained by Michael Patrick (Fenwick & West), the analysis of multiple sizes in the dataset is restricted to senior rounds because multiples are hard to justify and therefore infrequently used in pari passu rounds (i.e. only in cases where the company has so much existing senior Liquidation Preferences that a new investor cannot expect a sufficient return based on simple Liquidation Preference).

3.1.3 Optional Conversion Rights

The Optional Conversion Right enables holders of convertible preferred stock (or convertible debt) to force the company to replace their preferred shares with common shares, at any time before expiration (which is the earliest date of a Redemption, a (Deemed) Liquidation Event, or a Qualified Public Offering), and at a preset conversion ratio.[15] Formally, Optional Conversion generates an American-type call option on common shares of the company.

The payoff function can be described as a position of α *long call with* $E = 0$, which corresponds to the investor's pro rata share (fully diluted). The number of common shares receivable after conversion equals:

$$N^{c}_{vc_1}(t_i) = N^{p}_{vc_1}(t_i) * P(t_0)/C_{vc_1}(t_i)$$

The variables $N^{p}_{vc_1}(t_i)$ and $C_{vc_1}(t_i)$ are affected by the terms of Preemption rights, Anti-dilution rights and Pay-to-play provisions as described in Section 3.2.

Although VC investors are formally allowed to convert at any time before expiry, they will exercise this option only shortly before an anticipated exit transaction, when they can evaluate whether the exit proceeds receivable after conversion compensate for the loss of preferred rights. Thus, Optional Conversion is effectively exercised upon the occurrence of

[15] A model provision for Optional Conversion is provided in the NVCA Certificate of Incorporation (standard), pp. 15-16, and the NVCA Term Sheet, p. 4.

a Liquidation Event or a Sale of the Company.[16]

Since this study focuses on the effective use of covenants (which may differ from their formal specification), the option embedded in Optional Conversion is defined as a European-type option.

Proposition 3 (Optional Conversion) *The Optional Conversion Right generates a European-type call option on common shares of the company, which becomes exercisable upon the occurrence of the earliest of a Liquidation Event or Company Sale, that is at*

$$T_{OC} = T_{LP} = \begin{cases} \tau_{LE} & \textit{if}\, \tau_{IPO} > \tau_{LE} > 0, \textit{or if}\, \tau_{LE} > 0 \wedge \tau_{IPO} = 0 \\ \tau_{CS} & \textit{if}\, \tau_{IPO} = \tau_{LE} = 0. \end{cases}$$

The payoff function generated by Optional Conversion is:

$$\Pi_{OC}(T_{OC}, P(T_{OC})) = N^c_{vc_1}(T_{OC}) * P(T_{OC}) = \alpha(T_{OC}) * V(T_{OC})$$

The value of the option at $t \leq T_{OC}$ is:

$$F_{OC}(t, P_t) = e^{-r(T_{OC}-t)} E^*_t[\Pi_{OC}(T_{OC}, P(T_{OC})) - I(T_{OC}, P(T_{OC}))]$$

16 Theoretically, Optional Conversion is also relevant in the event of a Public Offering which does *not* fulfill the conditions of a "Qualified Public Offering". However, these non-qualified offerings are excluded in this model, since an IPO always meets the QPO conditions.

3.1.4 Interaction of Optional Conversion and Liquidation

By definition, convertible preferred stock generates *mutually exclusive* options, as Conversion into common shares brings about the loss of all preferred rights. In the NVCA model documents, this mutual exclusiveness is described as follows:[17]

> All shares of series A preferred stock which shall have been surrendered for conversion shall no longer be deemed to be outstanding and all rights with respect to such shares shall immediately cease and terminate at the time of conversion, except the right of the holders to receive shares of common stock in exchange therefore and to receive payment of any dividends declared but unpaid thereon.

Hence, in anticipation of a Liquidation Event or a Company Sale, the VC investor has the following decision choice:

1. Convert his preferred shares into common shares and earn his pro-rata share of the exit proceeds.
2. Keep his preferred shares and receive the liquidation amount.

The VC effectively holds a chooser option, which allows him to earn the maximum payoff from these alternative decisions. The payoff diagram for this option is illustrated in Figure 6 at the example of non-participating

[17] NVCA Certificate of Incorporation (standard), p. 17.

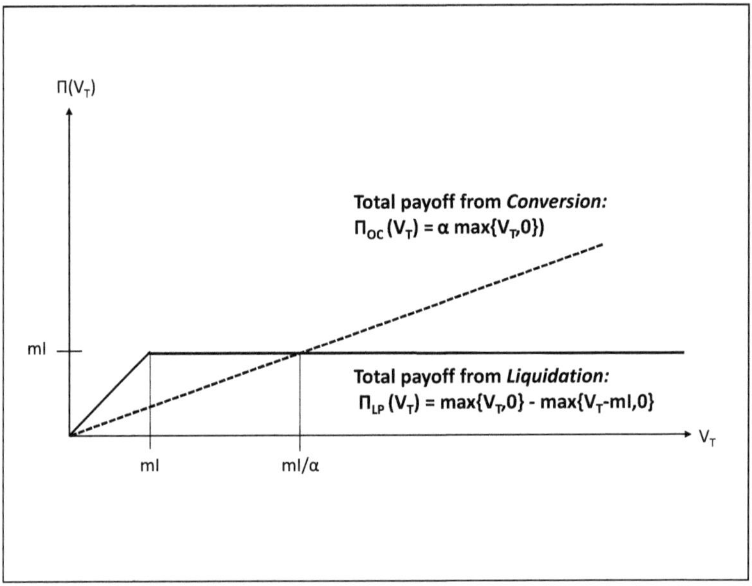

Figure 6: Payoff diagram for liquidation versus optional conversion

preferred stock. Optional Conversion yields payoffs below the liquidation amount (mI) for exit values below the indifference value (mI/α), while it yields payoffs above the liquidation amount for exit values above the indifference value. As explained earlier, the VC investor will make the conversion versus liquidation decision only shortly before the date of the Sale or Liquidation, when he has all information needed to compare the alternative payoffs. Thus, the chooser option generated by Optional Conversion and Liquidation rights is best described as a European-type option. This leads to the following proposition:

Proposition 4 (Liquidation Plus Optional Conversion) *Liquidation and Optional Conversion rights in interaction generate a European chooser option, which becomes exercisable upon the occurrence of the earliest of a Liquidation Event or a Sale of the Company. Hence the maturity of this option equals*

$$T_{LP} = \begin{cases} \tau_{LE} & \textit{if}\, \tau_{IPO} > \tau_{LE} > 0, \textit{or if}\, \tau_{LE} > 0 \wedge \tau_{IPO} = 0 \\ \tau_{CS} & \textit{if}\, \tau_{IPO} = \tau_{LE} = 0. \end{cases}$$

The pricing algorithm for this chooser option is derived from Gamba (2003). Let there be $H = 2$ mutually exclusive. These mutually exclusive options have payoffs Π_{LP} (from Liquidation), and Π_{OC} (from Optional Conversion) and the same (event-triggered) maturity $T = T_{LP} = T_{OC}$. The values of the two mutually exclusive options are defined as $F_{LP}(T, P_T)$ and $F_{OC}(T, P_T)$, respectively. Let $G(t, P_t)$ be the value of the opportunity to choose the best out of the options to convert or to obtain the liquidation amount. Define the control as ξ which takes values in the set $\{LP, OC\}$. $G(t, P_t)$ is then defined as follows:

$$G(t, P_t) = \max_{\xi}\{e^{-r(T-t)}E_t^*[F_\xi(T, P_T)]\}$$

The optimal exercise decisions and the corresponding payoffs of the chooser option embedded in Liquidation (without Participation) and Optional Conversion rights are provided in Table 1.

In a multiple round, multiple investors setting, the trade-off becomes more complex. The option holder still has the right to convert his preferred shares into common, but his payoff from conversion will depend on whether or not the remaining investors decide to convert as well. If all preferred holders as a group decide to convert, VC_1 receives his pro-rata share of the full exit proceeds. If the group of investors decides not to convert, VC_1 receives the pro-rata share of the proceeds remaining after distribution of liquidation preferences to other investors. Hence, the decision to convert for VC_1 will depend on the conversion decision taken by the group of preferred holders. This is analyzed in further detail in Section 3.3.1.

Table 1: Chooser Option Held by the Series A Investor

Provision	Payoff	Exercise Conditions	Exercise Restrictions
Conversion	$\Pi_{OC}(T)$	$\Pi_{OC}(T) \geq \Pi_{LP}(T)$	for $T = T_{LP} = T_{OC}$
Liquidation	$\Pi_{LP}(T)$	$\Pi_{LP}(T) \geq \Pi_{OC}(T)$	for $T = T_{LP} = T_{OC}$

3.2 Provisions Influencing the Number of Shares

A major consideration of VC investors when investing in a company is to anticipate how new rounds of financing required to fund the growth of the company until the exit transaction will affect the value of their shareholdings.[18] Therefore, at the time of investment, they have to assess how the issuance of additional shares in future financing rounds will dilute their ownership in the portfolio company over time, and to seek contractual protection against this dilutive effect. Dilution may take the form of *percentage dilution* (a decrease in the percentage of the entity an investor owns), or *economic dilution* (a decrease in the economic value of his investment in the entity). While economic dilution has a *direct* impact on the value of an investor's holdings, percentage dilution may have an important *indirect* value impact by altering non-economic features such as veto rights and other control rights. As shown in the following, Preemption rights are designed to protect the investor against percentage dilution, while Anti-dilution rights protect him against economic dilution. In the presence of Pay-to-play provisions, Preemption or Anti-dilution rights (or both) become contingent on the investor's participation in future rounds. Hence, protection from dilution comes at the cost of participation in future rounds.

---

18 See Wilmerding (2006), pp. 93-94.

3.2.1 Preemption Rights

The Preemption right (also called "right of first offer" or "right to participate pro rata in future rounds") represents a so-called "informal staging" mechanism, as it allows the VC investor to expand his holdings at any new financing round, whereby the terms are renegotiated at every round based on the future performance of the portfolio company and the bargaining power of the contracting parties.[19] More precisely, the investor may participate in future share issues up to his percentage interest in the company immediately before the round (or more if there are several rounds of allocation and other holders of this right do not fully exercise it), and is thereby fully protected against percentage dilution of his holdings.[20] Assuming a single round of allocation, the VC investor can purchase any portion ρ_1 of newly offered securities, which is inferior or equal to his pro-rata ownership percentage α in effect immediately before the new issue (on a fully-diluted basis). In this case, the number of preferred shares held after exercise of his Preemption right, $t_i < \tau_{exit}$, is defined as:

$$N^p_{vc_1}(t_i) = N^p_{vc_1}(t_{i-1}) + \rho_1(N^p_{VC}(t_i) - N^p_{VC}(t_{i-1}))$$

19 Due to their status of "insider" investors, existing investors usually have a substantial information advantage compared to external investors, which enables them to influence the terms of external rounds; they also have substantial bargaining power towards management, which allows them to lead internal rounds at attractive valuations if they can provide the necessary funding.

20 A model description of the Preemption right is provided in the NVCA Investors' Rights Agreement, pp. 23-25, and NVCA Term Sheet, p. 9.

with $\rho_1 \in [0, \alpha(t_{i-1})]$ and $\alpha(t_{i-1}) = (N^c_{vc_1}(t_{i-1}))/(N^c_{tot}(t_{i-1}))$.

In the case of multiple rounds of allocation, the investor's participation may exceed his pro-rata share, up to a maximum portion ρ_2, which equals the total ownership percentage of existing investors (on a fully-diluted basis) immediately before the new issue (and reflecting the case where none of the remaining preferred holders would exercise his Preemption right). In this scenario, the number of preferred shares held by the VC investor after exercise of his Preemption right equals:

$$N^p_{vc_1}(t_i) = N^p_{vc_1}(t_{i-1}) + \rho_2(N^p_{tot}(t_i) - N^p_{tot}(t_{i-1}))$$

with $\rho_2 \in [0, \beta(t_{i-1})]$ and $\beta(t_{i-1}) = (N^c_{VC}(t_{i-1}))/(N^c_{tot}(t_{i-1}))$.

3.2.2 Anti-dilution Rights

Anti-dilution protection allows an investor to limit the economic dilution of his investment in a company without being required to commit more capital over time (see Woronoff and Rosen, 2005b, p. 9). Anti-dilution protection is found in nearly 99% of the sample financings in the Fenwick & West dataset. Generally, Anti-dilution clauses protect preferred holders against dilution resulting from the following corporate events:

- cheap issuances of additional common stock or deemed additional common stock (in the form of common stock purchase rights, warrants, or securities convertible into common stock);

- structural changes in equity securities, including stock dividends, stock splits and reverse stock splits, as well as other distributions.[21]

The analysis will focus on protection mechanisms against dilution from cheap issuances of additional equity securities, since structural changes are not related to the performance of the company, and their inclusion adds no value to the pricing model (see Section 2.3.5).

Cheap issuances are issues of additional equity securities at a price per share inferior to the applicable conversion price in effect immediately prior to such issue. Hence, Anti-dilution protection becomes applicable in "down rounds". Typically, there are two types of (conversion price) Anti-dilution formulas: full ratchet and weighted average.

Full ratchet Anti-dilution protection reduces the preferred holder's conversion price to the share price applicable at the new round:[22]

$$C_{vc_1}(t_i) = P(t_i)$$

with

$C_{vc_1}(t_i)$: conversion price applicable to the preferred shares held by VC_1 after full-ratchet anti-dilution adjustment at t_i; and

$P(t_i)$: purchase price paid in the new round at t_i.

[21] Including those related to mergers and consolidations; extraordinary distributions of cash and property; sales of all or substantially all of the company's assets, followed by a distribution of the sale proceeds in the form of cash or property; recapitalizations; and common stock buybacks.

[22] See NVCA, Certificate of Incorporation (standard), p. 24; NVCA Term Sheet, p. 5.

This mechanism fully protects the investor against economic dilution from initial investment, as the securities receivable upon conversion after the adjustment will have the same aggregate value as the initial investment. At the same time, however, it fully shifts the costs of any decline in value to common shareholders. For this reason, this type of anti-dilution protection is used more rarely than weighted average protection.

Weighted average Anti-dilution protection reduces the preferred holder's conversion price to the weighted average price per share of securities issued both prior to and in the dilutive issuance, in accordance with the following formula:[23]

$$
\begin{aligned}
C_{vc_1}(t_i) &= C_{vc_1}(t_{i-1}) \times \frac{N^c_{tot}(t_{i-1}) + N^{c*}_{new}(t_i)}{N^c_{tot}(t_{i-1}) + N^c_{new}(t_i)} \\
&= \frac{C_{vc_1}(t_{i-1}) \times N^c_{tot}(t_{i-1}) + I_{new}(t_i)}{N^c_{tot}(t_{i-1}) + N^c_{new}(t_i)}
\end{aligned}
$$

Hereby, the parameters are defined as follows:

$C_{vc_1}(t_i)$: conversion price in effect after adjustment for dilution;

$C_{vc_1}(t_{i-1})$: conversion price in effect immediately prior to the dilutive issue (after all prior adjustments);

$N^c_{tot}(t_{i-1})$: number of shares of common stock outstanding immediately prior to the dilutive issue of common stock;

$N^c_{new}(t_i)$: number of additional shares of common stock issued (or deemed issued) in such transaction;

23 See NVCA Certificate of Incorporation (standard), p. 23; NVCA Term Sheet, p. 4.

$N^{c*}_{new}(t_i)$: number of shares of common stock that would have been issued (or deemed issued) if such shares had been issued at a price per share equal to $C_{vc_1}(t_{i-1})$, determined by dividing the aggregate consideration $I_{new}(t_i) = N^c_{new}(t_i) * P(t_i)$ received by the company in respect of such issue by $C_{vc_1}(t_{i-1})$.

The relative price contributions to arrive at the new conversion price can be weighed in several ways, depending on which shares to consider as outstanding, that is on which shares to include in $N^c_{tot}(t_{i-1})$:[24]

- The "Broad-based" or "California" interpretation accounts for all common stock outstanding on a fully-diluted basis (assuming the exercise or conversion of all warrants, options, and convertible securities outstanding immediately prior to the dilutive issue), which means that the preferred is seen to own less of the company prior to the dilutive issuance.

- The "Narrow-based" or "East Coast" interpretation excludes certain shares from the calculation of shares outstanding, for example all convertible securities that are out-of-the-money, or simply all shares of common stock issuable on conversion of options, warrants (and, potentially, even the preferred stock itself), whether they are in-the-money or not.

As the shares outstanding prior to the dilutive issuance are valued higher in the formula, the more shares considered outstanding (and hence the

24 See NVCA Certificate of Incorporation (standard), p. 23.

broader the base) prior to the dilutive issuance, the better off the unprotected shareholders (the common holders) and the worse off the holders of protected convertible securities (the preferred holders). Thus, the narrow-based interpretation can be understood as the more investor-favorable approach, while the broad-based approach is more company-favorable.

With the weighted average approach, losses from the value decrease are distributed among all holders of securities, and not born exclusively by the holders of common shares. This may not be the accurate way, but the best solution the parties can hope for, as the true cause of the drop in value cannot be clearly determined. For this reason, weighted average is the most commonly used type of Anti-dilution protection in the U.S.[25] This is confirmed by the Fenwick & West dataset, since 94% of Anti-dilution provisions use the weighted average formula.[26] Moreover, full ratchet provisions provided for in the initial contract often flip into weighted average provisions at later investment rounds.[27]

Independently of the chosen protection mechanism, the cost of anti-dilution protection granted to VC investors is partially born by the founders and the management. Thus, in cases where the continued involvement and motivation of these groups is crucial, investors only insist on exercising their anti-dilution rights up to a certain point. Beyond this point, they will expand the employee stock option plan or stop exercising their Anti-

25 See TR, 2009, p. 55.

26 As indicated by Hassan Sohbi (Taylor Wessing), the predominance of weighted average also applies to European contracting practices.

27 See Bagley & Dauchy (2008).

dilution rights, to prevent the ownership percentage of common holders from dropping below a minimum level of $10 - 15\%$.[28]

Anti-dilution provisions do not generate option value in isolation. However, they may alter embedded option values, since reducing the conversion price of preferred shares increases the number of common shares receivable by the investor upon conversion and consequently his final payoff. Technically, Anti-dilution rights add *strong path-dependency* to the option pricing problem. The number of shares receivable upon conversion becomes dependent on a property of the path followed by the underlying asset, namely on whether the price per share paid at the new financing round is inferior to the conversion price in effect immediately prior to this round. This can be captured in this model by adding a new independent variable in the form of $C_{vc_1}(t_{i-1})$, which is the conversion price in effect immediately before the new issue. The value of embedded options must then be described as $F(t, P(t), C_{vc_1}(t_{i-1}))$.

In practice, a company issues multiple series of preferred shares to multiple investors over time. The conversion price of shares belonging to a newly issued series is initially set equal to the purchase price of these shares, and then adapted over time as imposed by the Anti-dilution protection mechanism in place. Therefore, the conversion price variable must be tracked separately for each series of preferred shares. This is further elaborated in section 3.4, which derives the comprehensive pricing model.

28 This tradeoff is emphasized in Wilmerding (2006). As explained by Hassan Sohbi (Taylor Wessing), a similar rationale is applied by European VC investors.

3.2.3 Pay-to-play Penalties and Interaction Effects

Generally, Pay-to-play provisions (also called "Play-or-lose") are clauses, which penalize the VC investor for not fully participating in future "Qualified Financings" (unless a minimum percentage of preferred holders elects otherwise), by forcing him to convert all his preferred shares (or the applicable portion of his preferred shares)[29] into common shares or to forgo certain preferred rights. Hereby, Qualified Financings are defined as Share Issues, which result in a minimum amount of gross proceeds and in the reduction of the conversion price applicable to the relevant series of preferred shares. The penalties may take different degrees, ranging from forfeiture of Anti-dilution protection, Registration rights or Preemption rights, to Mandatory Conversion of preferred shares into shadow preferred shares or common shares, and loss of Board rights.[30]

Pay-to-play provisions are found in only 12% of the sample financings in the Fenwick & West dataset. However, this figure does not cover increasingly used "pull up" provisions, which have a similar economic effect than pay-to-play provisions, but which are defined in separate contractual agreements and not in the charter.[31] In Europe, the contractual specifica-

---

29 This portion equals the number of shares obtained by multiplying the aggregate number of shares of preferred stock held by such holder immediately prior to the Qualified Financing by a fraction, the numerator of which is equal to the amount (if positive) by which such holder's pro-rata amount exceeds the number of offered securities actually purchased by such holder in such Qualified Financing, and the denominator of which is equal to such holder's pro-rata amount.

30 See NVCA Term Sheet (pp. 5-6).

31 This comment is provided in the Fenwick & West Quarterly Reports 2009.

tion of Pay-to-play penalties is even less frequent, but both the (ex-ante) incentive effect and the (ex-post) penalty effect are often replicated informally, due to the bargaining power of incoming investors. On the one hand, incoming investors often require existing investors to participate in the new round as a key pre-condition to invest (and often even to look in depth at the investment opportunity) or as a major influence factor of contract terms (e.g. the lack of participation of old investors may cause a steep valuation discount or a loss of rights such as anti-dilution, veto rights, etc.). On the other hand, incoming investors will usually ask that their shares bear more senior rights than the shares of existing investors. This sometimes forces old investors to reduce their protection levels by foregoing certain rights, such as Liquidation Preference, Anti-dilution protection (usually for the consecutive financing round) or veto rights (indirectly, via shift in their percentage ownership).[32]

The most onerous version of Pay-to-play penalties in the U.S. is mandatory conversion into common stock, which represents 78% of the Pay-to-Play provisions found in the Fenwick & West sample rounds. In essence, this penalty ends any preferential rights tied to the converted shares, including the right to participate pro rata in future financings and the right to influence management decisions.[33]

The alternative version of the Pay-to-play penalty forces non-participating investors to convert their shares into so-called "shadow" preferred, which

---

32 As commented by Hassan Sohbi (Taylor Wessing).

33 See NVCA Certificate of Incorporation (standard), p. 29.

differs from the original preferred stock in the following aspects:[34]

- the conversion price is fixed at the conversion price in effect immediately prior to the financing and will not be subject to any further anti-dilution adjustment (applying in the case of cheap issuances of additional common stock);
- the new series will not include an analogous provision on Special Mandatory Conversion; and
- the terms of this series may vary from the terms of the series A preferred stock to the extent deemed necessary by the Board of Directors to accomplish the intent of this provision.

Hence, the VC investor loses some, but not all preferred rights. For example, he may lose his Anti-dilution protection and Preemption right, but keep the remaining rights including protective provisions and board voting rights.

According to the NVCA, conversion into common stock is preferable to conversion into shadow preferred because (a) it represents a harsher penalty (and is hence more effective at forcing the investor to participate in future rounds); (b) it facilitates future charter amendments, since the latter do not require the approval of common shareholders, whereas they may require the approval of the holders of a majority of shadow preferred

34 See NVCA Certificate of Incorporation (with Pay-to-Play lite), pp. 29-30.

stock (e.g. for Delaware law); and (c) it avoids the complexities associated with the creation of the shadow series of preferred stock.[35]

When planning an investment, VC investors broadly estimate how much funding the company will need to raise in the future and at which valuations, based on its cash-flow requirements and likely exit scenarios. Hence, they anticipate the potential dilution effect from future rounds and reserve a certain amount of funding (on average three or four times the first investment) to exercise their Preemption rights (see Wilmerding, 2006, p. 53).[36] Moreover, VC investors are acutely aware of signaling effects: if existing investors do not fully participate in a future round, this deters potential new investors from entering the deal. The participation incentive increases even further in the presence of Pay-to-play penalties, since investors will not incur the risk of losing their Preemption rights, Antidilution protection, or even all preferred rights. This is confirmed by the Fenwick & West dataset, since less than 5% of the sample rounds brought about reorganizations in the form of conversion of preferred shares into junior stock (whether shadow preferred or common stock). Based on these arguments, the author makes the following simplifying assumption:

35 See NVCA Certificate of Incorporation (with Pay-to-play lite), p. ii.

36 This also holds true for European investors, as confirmed by Hassan Sohbi (Taylor Wessing).

Assumption 4 (Full Exercise of Preemption Rights) *VC Investors fully exercise their Preemption rights at any future financing round and hence maintain their pro-rata ownership percentage as well as their preferred rights over time.*

Assuming full exercise of Preemption rights by all holders of this right (and hence one single round of distribution), the number of shares held by VC_1 after financing round i equals, for all t_i with $t_0 < t_i < \tau_{exit}$:

$$N^p_{vc_1,p}(t_i) = N^p_{vc_1,p}(t_{i-1}) + \alpha(t_{i-1})(N^p_{tot}(t_i) - N^p_{tot}(t_{i-1}))$$

with $\alpha(t_{i-1}) = N^c_{vc_1}(t_{i-1})/(N^c_{tot}(t_{i-1}))$.
The cumulated investment of VC_1 after round i is:

$$I_{vc_1}(t_i) = I_{vc_1}(t_{i-1}) + \alpha(t_{i-1})(N^p_{tot}(t_i) - N^p_{tot}(t_{i-1}))P(t_i)$$

To limit the complexity of the model, the total number of participants in future financing rounds is defined as follows:

Assumption 5 (Participants in Follow-on Rounds) *Participants in future financings include all existing investors as well as one new (external) investor per round.*

This implies that the number of participants (j) in any round (i) equals:

$$j = \begin{cases} i+1 & \text{if } t_i < t_{exit} \\ i & \text{if } t_i = t_{exit} \end{cases}$$

3.3 Provisions Granting Exercise Flexibilities to Preferred Holders

This chapter covers contractual rights, which allow the VC investor to directly or indirectly control the type and timing of exit. Control over exit is crucial for the VC business model, since different exit scenarios impact the size of exit proceeds, their allocation among the parties and final returns on investment (see Smith, 2005, p. 316).

3.3.1 Shareholder and Board Voting Rights

This chapter covers Board Voting rights and Shareholder Voting rights (collectively defined as "Control rights"), which allow the VC investor to initiate and decide upon major corporate actions. Since Control rights are prescribed by corporation law, they are defined in accordance with the revised Model Business Corporation Act (MBCA), which provides the basis for corporation law in the majority of U.S. states.[37]

3.3.1.1 Board Voting Rights

The Board of Directors is responsible for hiring, evaluating and firing top management, for advising and ratifying general corporate strategies and

[37] The MBCA represents a *model* state incorporation statute that was prepared by the American Bar Association's Committee on Corporate Laws for adoption by state legislatures, with the purpose of improving the rationality of U.S. corporation law. It was completely revised in 1984.

decisions in the ordinary course of its business, for filling vacancies on the board and, most importantly in this context, for initiating certain corporate actions including financing and exit events. The composition of the Board of Directors varies from company to company. The author relies on a general model of Board composition, which is aligned with results of empirical studies (see Kaplan and Strömberg, 2003; Smith, 2005) as well as the NVCA model documents.[38] According to this model, the Board seats are allocated as follows:

1. A specified number of Board seats (n_p) are allocated to the holders of each series (or multiple series voting together) of preferred stock.
2. A specified number of Board seats (n_c) are allocated to the holders of common stock.
3. Any remaining board seats (n_r) are filled by
   - Directors elected by the holders of preferred stock and the holders of common stock *voting together as a single class*; *or*

[38] The NVCA model documents contain two conflicting provisions on the composition of the Board: the Certificate of Incorporation prescribes that the remaining Directors be voted by common and preferred holders together as a single class, while the Voting Agreement foresees that these seats be filled by independent directors. See NVCA Certificate of Incorporation (standard), pp. 12-13 and NVCA Voting Agreement, pp. 3-4. Since a company would generally not want to have two conflicting provisions within the same contractual framework, we assume that this inconsistency between the documents is unintended, and present the described scenarios as two *alternative* scenarios.

- independent Directors, which are *mutually agreed upon* by the common and preferred shareholders.

The total board structure of a portfolio company can then be described as $n_{tot} = n_p + n_c + n_r$ and reflects one of the following control scenarios:

- *Investor Control* if $n_p > n_c + n_r$;
- *Entrepreneur Control* if $n_c > n_p + n_r$;
- *Contingent Control* if $n_p = n_c$ and the tie-breaking vote(s) is (are) held by n_r directors that are elected by common and preferred holders voting as a single class. Over time, this vote can tip the balance of power to one side or the other. At any specific point in time, however, only one party controls the board vote and Contingent Control is effectively equivalent to:
  - *Investor Control*, if $\beta(t_i) > 50\%$; or
  - *Entrepreneur Control*, if $\beta(t_i) \leq 50\%$

  where β is the (fully-diluted) ownership percentage of preferred stock holders.
- *Joint Control* where $n_p = n_c$ and the tie-breaking vote(s) is (are) held by n_r independent Director(s), who act(s) in the interest of the company. Here, Board Control can shift towards the VC investor or the entrepreneur at any vote, depending on who's interest is more

closely aligned with the company interest for the item subject to vote.

Over time, board composition tends to move from Entrepreneur Control to Investor Control, as VC investors usually gain additional board seats with each round of investment (either by bargaining or by acquiring a majority ownership stake). The pricing model derived in this thesis focuses on the case of Contingent Control, since this board structure reflects common practices in the U.S and accommodates the automatic transfer of control over time, in alignment with changes in the shareholder structure. Under this assumption, knowledge about the shareholder structure provides full knowledge about the scenario of board control.

3.3.1.2 Stockholder Voting Rights

Stockholder voting rights are the rights of holders of preferred and common stock to vote on major corporate actions within the scope of (ordinary or extraordinary) Shareholder Meetings (see TR, 2009, p. 68). Shareholder decisions typically require simple majority of votes, or sometimes a super-majority (if so prescribed by the statute, articles of association, bylaws, or shareholder voting agreements).
Matters subject to vote in Shareholder Meetings include, among others:

- Election and removal of directors (vote by classes of shares)
- Fundamental corporate changes (in the structure or business of the

corporation), including:

  - Amendments of the Articles of Incorporation (e.g. increase in the number of authorized shares or reduction of dividend rights of preferred holders)[39]
  - Merger (excluding short-form mergers, provided the parent corporation holds 90% of the subsidiary's shares)
  - Consolidation
  - Share exchange
  - Sale of all or substantially all of the assets
  - (Voluntary) Dissolution and Liquidation

- Adoption and amendment of bylaws.

For simplification, it will be assumed that the above matters are subject to simple majority vote. The party possessing simple voting majority can then decide on all matters subject to shareholder vote including the exit strategy and timing.

Accordingly, at any time step, $t_i \in [t_0, t_N]$, the shareholder structure defines one of the two following scenarios of Voting Control:

---

[39] Since IPOs inevitably require an amendment of the company's Articles of Incorporation, the right to prevent such amendment provides effective control over the timing of the IPO. In Europe, legal frameworks typically prescribe that share issues, share transfers and IPOs be also listed as separate voting items (as commented by Hassan Sohbi from Taylor Wessing).

- VC Voting Control: the group of all preferred holders has more than 50% of the voting rights, that is, $\beta > 50\%$;
- Founder Voting Control: the group of all common holders has 50% or more of the voting rights (e.g. in early stage investments), that is, if $\beta \leq 50\%$.

To assess the impact of Control rights on embedded option prices, the author makes the simplifying assumption that preferred holders act in common interest with regard to exit decisions, and hence that they take exit decisions as a group.[40]

As Voting Control also infers Board Control, the group of preferred holders gains full control over the exit event when it obtains majority ownership of the company (if $\beta > 50\%$). The time step at which this switch of control occurs is defined as: $\tau_{contr} = \inf\{t_i : \beta > 50\%\}$. Hence, if no exit event has occurred before τ_{contr}, the exit date as well as the choice of the exit scenario are controlled by the group of Preferred Holders. This affects embedded options as follows:

Proposition 5 (Direct Control Rights) *In the presence of Control rights, if $\tau_{contr} \leq \tau_{exit}$, the type and timing of exit are not determined by path-*

40 In practice, the interests of different preferred holders are not fully aligned, since they hold different series of preferred stock with different rights, and usually represent multiple VC funds (with distinct lifetimes, return expectations, stage focus and industry focus). This conflict of interest among preferred holders could be accounted for in a game-theoretical analysis, which exceeds the scope of this thesis but represents an interesting path for future research.

dependent trigger events, but reflect optimal exercise policies of the group of preferred holders in the exercise period $[\tau_{contr}, t_N]$.

Board and Voting Control allows the group of preferred holders to choose among IPO or Sale of the Company, and to control the date of the transaction (in the time interval providing this exercise flexibility). Depending on the chosen exit event, they have the following alternatives:

- *Sale of the Company*: in this exit scenario, they may either convert their preferred shares into common or keep their preferred shares and sell them to the buyer (or partner in case of a merger).

- *IPO*: this scenario is only possible if the pre-offer company valuation is equal or superior to the $\$200m$ threshold; when the preferred holders opt for this scenario, their shares are automatically converted into common and sold to the public after expiration of the lockup period.

- *Wait or defer the exit*: if the payoff from continuation (that is from exiting at a later point in time) is superior to the proceeds from exiting at the current time step, the Preferred Holders will defer the exit until the optimal date.

If, at any time step in the given interval, the share value falls below the liquidation threshold (see Section 2.3.5), the company is assumed to go bankrupt and the above options are not available.

The author defines τ_{exit}^{contr} the path-wise optimal stopping time with respect to the information generated by P_{t_k} restricted to the discrete set of possible exercise dates $K_p^{contr}(\omega_p; \tau_{contr}, t_N)$, which fulfill the exercise restrictions. The solution to the optimal stopping problem is then obtained using the Bellman equation of the optimal stopping problem in discrete time:

$$H(t_k, P_{t_k}) = \max_{t_k \in K^{contr}} \{\max_{\xi,\psi}\{\Phi_{\xi,\psi}(t_k, P(t_k))\}, W(t_k, P(t_k))\}$$

Hereby, $W(t_k, P(t_k))$ is the continuation value (or value of waiting), defined as:

$$W(t_k, P(t_k)) = e^{-r(t_{k+1}-t_k)} E_{t_k}^{\star}[H(t_{k+1}, P(t_{k+1}))]$$

with $W(t_N, P(t_N)) = 0$ and $\max_{\xi,\psi}\{\Phi_{\xi,\psi}(t_k, P(t_k))\}$ is the maximum *net payoff* (after deduction of the cumulated investment cost to the group of preferred holders) from the alternative exit decisions at t_k, whereby $\xi_{t_k} = \{IPO, CS\}$ is the set of possible exit scenarios and $\psi_{t_k,\xi_{t_k}}$ is the set of alternative actions contingent on the exit scenarios:

$$\psi_{t_k,\xi_{t_k}} = \begin{cases} AC & \text{if } \xi_{t_k} = IPO \\ OC, LP & \text{if } \xi_{t_k} = CS \end{cases}$$

To allow for the comparison of all alternative net payoffs at the same time step t_k, the net payoff from Mandatory Conversion at IPO obtained after expiration of the lockup period must be discounted back to t_k. Hence,

$$\Phi_{MC}(t_k) = e^{-r(T_{MC}-t_k)}\Phi_{MC}(T_{MC})$$

where $T_{MC} = \inf\{t_i : t_i \geq \tau_{IPO} + 0,5\}$ and $\Phi_{MC}(T_{MC})$ is the net payoff that would be obtained by the group of preferred holders at T_{MC}, that is after expiration of the lockup period.

Table 2: Chooser Option Held by the Group of VC Investors With Control Rights

Exit Event	Action	Group Payoff	Exercise Conditions	Exercise Restrictions
IPO	convert	$\Phi_{MC}(t_k)$	$\Phi_{MC}(t_k) \geq \Phi_{LP}(t_k)$ and $\Phi_{MC}(t_k) \geq \Phi_{OC}(t_k)$ and $\Phi_{MC}(t_k) \geq W(t_k)$	for $t_k \in [\tau_{contr}, t_N]$ and $t_k < \tau_{LE}$ and $V_{pre}(t_k) \geq h_{IPO}$ and $T_{MC} \leq t_N$
Sale	convert	$\Phi_{OC}(t_k)$	$\Phi_{OC}(t_k) \geq \Phi_{LP}(t_k)$ and $\Phi_{OC}(t_k) \geq \Phi_{MC}(t_k)$ and $\Phi_{OC}(t_k) \geq W(t_k)$	for $t_k \in [\tau_{contr}, t_N]$ and $t_k < \tau_{LE}$
Sale	do not convert	$\Phi_{LP}(t_k)$	$\Phi_{LP}(t_k) \geq \Phi_{OC}(t_k)$ and $\Phi_{LP}(t_k) \geq \Phi_{MC}(t_k)$ and $\Phi_{LP}(t_k) \geq W(t_k)$	for $t_k \in [\tau_{contr}, t_N]$ and $t_k < \tau_{LE}$
No exit	continue	0	otherwise	for $t_k \in [\tau_{contr}, t_N]$ and $t_k < \tau_{LE}$

Note: $\Phi_{\psi}(t_k)$ is the net payoff function for the group of preferred holders; $W(t_k)$ is the continuation value at stopping time $t_k \in K_p^{contr}$.

The trade-off between alternative exit scenarios and continuation is presented in Table 3. If, for any t_k, the payoff from any particular exit scenario is both equal or superior to the payoff from alternative exit scenarios *and* equal or superior to the continuation value, then the groups of preferred holders initiate an exit transaction at this date and $\tau_{exit}^{contr} = t_k$. The optimal stopping time is found by recursive application of the decision rule described above, proceeding backward from the latest possible exercise date to the earliest possible exercise date. At some previous step of this procedure, if $\tau_{exit}^{contr} > t_k$, and the above exercise condition holds at the current step t_k, the stopping time along path ω is updated to $\tau_{exit}^{contr} = t_k$. The adjusted exit date $\tau_{exit}^{\star}$, which accounts for path-dependent exit events and for the presence of Control rights, is then defined as follows (for any simulation path ω):

$$\begin{array}{ll} \text{If } \tau_{exit} < \tau_{contr} & \text{then } \tau_{exit}^{\star} = \tau_{exit} \\ \text{If } \tau_{exit} \geq \tau_{contr} \wedge \exists t_k \in K & \text{then } \tau_{exit}^{\star} = \tau_{exit}^{contr} \end{array}$$

Depending on the optimal exit decision made by the group of preferred holders, the series A investor (VC_1) has the following options:

- *In the event of an IPO*: the investor's shares automatically convert into common and are sold to the public after the expiration of the lockup period.

- *In the event of a Company Sale*: if the preferred holders opt for conversion, the individual investor's shares will also convert and he will earn his pro-rata share of total exit proceeds; if the preferred holders vote against conversion, the individual investor may choose between receiving his liquidation amount or converting into common, whereby he would receive his pro-rata share of the proceeds remaining after payout of the Liquidation Preferences of his co-investors.

The following table illustrates the payoffs to VC_1 in accordance with the group decision of all Preferred Holders.

Table 3: Payoffs to VC_1 in the Presence of Control Rights

Exit Event	Action Group	Action VC_1	Payoff VC_1	Exercise Conditions VC_1
IPO	convert	convert	$\Pi_{MC}(t_k)$	
Sale	convert	convert	$\Pi_{OC}(t_k)$	
Sale	do not convert	do not convert	$\Pi_{LP}(t_k)$	$\Pi_{LP}(t_k) \geq \Pi_{OC}^{-}(t_k)$
		convert	$\Pi_{OC}^{-}(t_k)$	$\Pi_{OC}^{-}(t_k) \geq \Pi_{LP}(t_k)$

Note: $\Pi(t_k)$ is the net payoff function for VC_1 (with Π_{OC}^{-} defined as VC_1's pro-rata share of proceeds remaining after payout of the Liquidation Preferences of his co-investors), and t_k equals $\tau_{exit}^{\star}$ (as defined earlier).

3.3.2 Redemption, Demand Registration and Drag-along

3.3.2.1 Redemption Rights

Redemption rights formally allow the VC investor to ask that their preferred shares be repurchased by the company at a pre-defined price (equal or superior to the original price per share paid at investment) if no exit event has taken place within a certain time period.[41] This time period is usually defined as a minimum of five years after the investment date, and aligned with the anticipated exit horizon (see TR, 2009, p. 66). The Redemption Right is the only term, besides Liquidation Preference, which defines a contracted payment on which the company could default. This is especially relevant in situations in which the management objectives differ from the exit strategy and timing originally agreed upon with the investors (e.g. if the company would have the opportunity to realize a liquidity event but the founder opposes the transaction to stay in his position rather than supporting the transaction), and in so-called "sideways situations", where the company generates sufficient revenues and cash flow to maintain operations, but was not able to realize attractive exit scenarios in the anticipated time horizon.

In practice, Redemption rights raise a number of difficulties for the company and for investors. The company may find it harder to obtain new financing when redemption obligations are categorized as company debt.

[41] Model provisions are presented in the NVCA Certificate of Incorporation (standard), pp. 32-33, and the NVCA Term Sheet, p. 6.

Unless the company is performing particularly well, it does generally not have enough cash available to buy the investors out, or it may not be legally permitted to redeem shares (by reason of restrictions under Delaware law and other state corporate law).[42] To limit these exercise risks, VC investors sometimes require the company to create a *sinking fund* to ensure that sufficient capital would be available for the redemption, or they demand that certain *penalty provisions* apply if the company cannot pay the full Redemption Amount (e.g. payment of the redemption amount in the form of a one-year note to each unredeemed preferred holder, or entitlement of the preferred holders to elect a majority of the Company's Board of Directors until the redemption amount is paid back in full).

In the Fenwick & West dataset, Redemption rights are found in 27% of the sample financings. Due to the difficulties described above, VC investors rarely exercise them. However, the mere threat of exercise provides investors with additional leverage to force a liquidity event as soon as possible after the initially anticipated exit horizon. European investors rarely ask for a Redemption Right in the contract, and consider its exercise a measure of last resort. Instead, they rely on "mandatory exit rights", which represent truly *initiatory* exit rights.[43] As Redemption rights are rarely exercised, and, if exercised, do not guarantee payment of the full Redemption Amount, they are not modeled as a separate option in the

42 This explanation was provided by Michael Patrick (Fenwick & West).

43 As commented by Hassan Sohbi (Taylor Wessing).

pricing model. However, they generate value by indirectly allowing the preferred holders to initiate an exit after a certain time period (at the initial date of the redemption right). This influences the exercise restrictions of options embedded in other rights.

3.3.2.2 Demand Registration

Demand Registration rights formally enable investors to require the company to register their shares for sale in a public offering upon the earliest of (a) a minimum number of years after the closing (typically three to five years), or (b) the expiration of the lock-up period after the IPO. Such registration must meet certain minimum conditions, defined as minimum anticipated net proceeds (at least one to five million dollars for Form S-3 Demand, respectively \$5 to \$15 million dollars for Form S-1 Demand) or a minimum percentage of outstanding Registrable Securities (20% to 100% for Form S-1 Demand).[44] The VC investor typically asks for the right to request at least two registrations, while the company tries to limit this number as far as possible (since the costs are mostly born by the company and not the investor).

Theoretically, if the VC investor has the right to make a demand, he can indirectly force the company to initiate a separate public offering. De facto, however, he cannot impose an IPO upon the other parties, as the cooperation of the founders and the management is an essential element

---

44 Model provisions are presented in the NVCA Investors' Rights Agreement, pp. 5-8, and the NVCA Term Sheet, p. 7.

of any IPO process (see Brobeck, 2003, p. 8). Moreover, the provision is not formally designed to provide investors with a right of initiation, since the effective date is usually postponed with each new investment round up to a point in time after the expected date of the IPO. For those reasons, Demand Registration should be interpreted as a protective exit right, which is rarely exercised in practice, but which provides investors with leverage in influencing the nature and timing of company-initiated registrations (via the impending deadline and not the impending threat of exit) or other exit events (see Smith, 2005, pp. 353-354).

Hence, as argued in the case of Redemption rights, Demand Registration will not be modeled as a separate option. Instead, the model will account for the fact that they allow the preferred holders to initiate an exit event, if such event has not taken place by the date at which the Registration right becomes effective.

3.3.2.3 Drag-along Rights

Drag-along rights (also called "Bring-along rights") constitute the contractual right of an investor to force all other shareholders to agree to a specific action, most commonly the Sale of the Company, and to participate in this transaction on the same terms as himself. This right is systematically granted to majority shareholders, and regularly also to VC investors with minority shareholdings.[45] Formally, it enables the VC investor to

[45] Model provisions are listed in the NVCA Voting Agreement, pp. 5-6, and in the NVCA Term Sheet, pp. 11-12.

initiate a Sale of the Company to a strategic buyer in a scenario where the exit through a public listing is difficult and where minority shareholders could block the transaction. Moreover, it allows him to offer the full company for sale (as opposed to his pro-rata share of the company), which is usually a precondition to attract strategic buyers (who are unlikely to be interested in a minority stake), and to obtain a "premium", which is an appreciation in the offer price resulting from a higher level of control over the company. In the U.S., Drag-along rights are typically provided for in later rounds, where there is growing concern that the parties may have diverging economic interests in the exit transaction.[46]

In practice, it is hard to force an exit without full cooperation of the management, because the buyer often requires continuous involvement of management as a prerequisite of the transaction, and because the transaction can only be finalized once all parties agree upon fair company value, which is not possible in the presence of diverging subjective views. Thus, the initiation of a Sale of the Company by preferred holders is not as straightforward as implied by the legal terms, and drag-along rights are rarely exercised (in the sense that the holder goes to the Courts to enforce the exit transaction). However, VC investors rely on the credible threat of exercising their Drag-along Right to indirectly force management to initiate exit via Sale of the Company or via IPO.[47]

---

46 Drag-along rights are not covered by the Fenwick & West dataset.

47 As clarified by Hassan Sohbi (Taylor Wessing), Drag-along rights are used for a similar purpose in Europe.

Again, this right is not modeled as a separate option. Instead, the author assumes that it reinforces the initiatory power of preferred holders with regard to an exit event and thereby impacts the exercise restrictions of other embedded options. This is formally described in the next chapter.

3.3.2.4 Synthesis for Initiatory Exit Rights

For illustrative purposes, the author assumes that Demand Registration, Drag-along rights, as well as Redemption rights become effective on the same date, t_{ant}, which reflects the anticipated exit date agreed upon by all parties at the time of contracting (with $t_{ant} < t_N$). Hence, the first time step with exercise flexibility induced by these rights is:

$$\tau_{ant} = \inf\{t_i : t_i \geq t_{ant}\}.$$

Similarly than for Control rights, the optimal exercise decisions of embedded options represent consensus decisions of the group of preferred holders. As opposed to Control rights, however, Exit rights only allow preferred holders to *initiate* the exit event (if the company has failed to do so in the anticipated exit horizon), but not to *defer* an exit event initiated by the company (when the barrier conditions are met). This imposes an additional restriction upon the set of possible exercise dates $t_k \in K^{init}$, in the form of $t_k < \tau_{exit}$. The impact of Exit rights on embedded option prices can be formally described as follows:

Proposition 6 (Exit Rights) *In the presence of initiatory Exit rights, if* $\tau_{ant} < \tau_{exit}$, *the type and timing of exit is not determined by path-dependent trigger events, but reflects optimal exercise decisions taken by the group of preferred holders in the exercise period* $[\tau_{ant}, \tau_{exit}[$.

Table 4 presents the trade-off (at each stopping time t_k and for each sample path ω) between (a) initiating alternative exit scenarios and (b) deferring the exit decision. The solution to the optimal decision problem is obtained as already explained in Section 3.3.1.

Table 4: Chooser Option Held by the Group of VC Investors With Exit Rights

Exit Event	Action	Payoff	Exercise Conditions	Exercise Restrictions
IPO	conversion (automatic)	$\Phi_{MC}(t_k)$	$\Phi_{MC}(t_k) \geq \Phi_{LP}(t_k)$ and $\Phi_{MC}(t_k) \geq \Phi_{OC}(t_k)$ and $\Phi_{MC}(t_k) \geq W(t_k)$	for $t_k \in [\tau_{ant}, t_N]$ and $t_k < \tau_{exit}$ and $V_{pre}(t_k) \geq h_{IPO}$ and $T_{MC} \leq t_N$
Sale	conversion (optional)	$\Phi_{OC}(t_k)$	$\Phi_{OC}(t_k) \geq \Phi_{LP}(t_k)$ and $\Phi_{OC}(t_k) \geq \Phi_{MC}(t_k)$ and $\Phi_{OC}(t_k) \geq W(t_k)$	for $t_k \in [\tau_{ant}, t_N]$ and $t_k < \tau_{exit}$
Sale	no conv.	$\Phi_{LP}(t_k)$	$\Phi_{LP}(t_k) \geq \Phi_{OC}(t_k)$ and $\Phi_{LP}(t_k) \geq \Phi_{MC}(t_k)$ and $\Phi_{LP}(t_k) \geq W(t_k)$	for $t_k \in [\tau_{ant}, t_N]$ and $t_k < \tau_{exit}$
No exit	continue	0	otherwise	$t_k \in [\tau_{ant}, t_N]$ and $t_k < \tau_{exit}$

Note: $\Phi_{\psi}(t_k)$ is the net payoff function for the group of preferred holders;
$W(t_i)$ is the continuation value at exercise date ($t_k \in K^{init}$).

3.4 Synthesis of the Contract Pricing Model

This section combines the findings from the previous sections to build the comprehensive pricing model, which derives option values for all provisions in interaction and accounts for multiple rounds with multiple investors and multiple series of preferred shares.

3.4.1 Exit Type and Timing

As defined in Sections 3.3.1 and 3.3.2, the preferred holders as a group gain influence over the type and timing of the exit transaction when they obtain Voting and Board Control, or when they can threaten to exercise their Redemption, Demand Registration or Drag-along rights. In the presence of both control and exit rights, the adjusted exit date $\tau_{exit}^{contr,init}$ is obtained by solving the optimal decision problem with the combined set of exercise dates $t_k \in (K^{contr} \cup K^{init})$.

$$\begin{aligned} &\text{If } \tau_{exit} \leq \tau_{ant} \wedge t_{exit} < \tau_{contr} \quad \text{then } \tau_{exit}^{\star} = \tau_{exit} \\ &\text{If } \tau_{exit} > \tau_{ant} \vee t_{exit} \geq \tau_{contr} \quad \text{then } \tau_{exit}^{\star} = \tau_{exit}^{contr,init} \end{aligned}$$

Hence, the exit transaction either reflects a path-dependent event (as defined in Section 2.3.5, or the optimal exercise decision of the group of preferred holders (as defined in Sections 3.3.1 and 3.3.2), depending on when the preferred holders obtain voting and board control, respectively when they can start exercising their exit rights. Any intermediary jump date t_i after the investment date and before the exit transaction (with $0 < t_i < \tau^{\star}_{exit}$) reflects a follow-on VC financing round, at which the company issues a new series of preferred shares. The following sections describe how the total number of shares held by investors evolves over these financing rounds.

3.4.2 Evolution of the Numbers of Shares

As derived in Section 3.2.2, the exercise of Anti-dilution rights leads to adjustments of conversion prices of preferred shares in the event of down rounds. In a multiple round setting, conversion prices must be tracked for each existing investor, vc_j, with $j = [1, i+1]$, and for all series of preferred stock $s \in [j, i+1]$ held by the respective investor at any time step before exit, $t_i < \tau^{\star}_{exit}$.

At the purchase date of the respective series, t_{s-1}, the conversion price simply equals the purchase price: $C_{vc_j,s}(t_{s-1}) = P(t_{s-1})$.
For all remaining jump dates before exit, with $t_{s-1} < t_i < \tau^{\star}_{exit}$, the conversion prices are adapted as follows:

If $P(t_i) \geq C_{vc_j,s}(t_{i-1})$

then $C_{vc_j,s}(t_i) = C_{vc_j,s}(t_{i-1})$

If $P(t_i) < C_{vc_j,s}(t_{i-1})$

$$\text{then } C_{vc_j,s}(t_i) = \begin{cases} P(t_i) \\ \text{(for full ratchet protection), or} \\ \frac{C_{vc_j}(t_{i-1}) \times N^c_{tot}(t_{i-1}) + I_{new}(t_i)}{N^c_{tot}(t_{i-1}) + N^c_{new}(t_i)} \\ \text{(for weighted average protection)} \end{cases}$$

The total number of common shares (on an as-converted basis and aggregated over all series of preferred shares) held by vc_j at t_{i-1} (immediately before round i) is obtained as follows:

$$\forall t_i \;/\; t_1 < t_i < \tau^\star_{exit} : \; N^c_{vc_j}(t_{i-1}) = \sum_{s=j}^{i} \left(N^p_{vc_j,s}(t_{i-1}) * \frac{P(t_{s-1})}{C_{vc_j,s}(t_{i-1})} \right)$$

As explained in Section 3.2.1, all existing investors (that is all investors who had participated in prior rounds) fully exercise their Preemption Right and participate in the new round i up to their pro-rata ownership percentage in effect immediately before this round. This percentage is obtained as follows:

$$\alpha_{vc_j}(t_{i-1}) = N^c_{vc_j}(t_{i-1}) / N^c_{tot}(t_{i-1})$$

with $N^c_{vc_j}$ as derived above.

The number of shares of the new series acquired by vc_j (with $j = [1, i{+}1]$) in the new round equals:

$$\forall t_i \;/\; t_0 < t_i < \tau^{\star}_{exit} : \; N^p_{vc_j,s}(t_i) = \alpha_{vc_j}(t_{i-1})(N^p_{tot}(t_i) - N^p_{tot}(t_{i-1}))$$

with α as derived above.

Finally, this allows for the calculation of the total number of preferred shares held by each existing investor after the new round:

$$N^p_{vc_j}(t_i) = N^p_{vc_j}(t_{i-1}) + \alpha_{vc_j}(t_{i-1})(N^p_{tot}(t_i) - N^p_{tot}(t_{i-1}))$$

3.4.3 Combined Payoff Functions

Based on the final exit date $\tau^{\star}_{exit}$ (which accounts for path-dependent trigger events, control rights and exit rights), one can derive the payoff to the Series A investor.

If the exit transaction is an IPO (that is if $\tau^{\star}_{exit} = \tau_{IPO}$), all preferred holders are obliged to convert their preferred shares into common and the series A investor receives the payoff from the forward contract generated by Mandatory Conversion in interaction with Piggyback Registration (see Section 3.1.1).

If the exit event is a Company Sale or Liquidation Event (that is if $\tau^{\star}_{exit} = \tau_{CS} \vee \tau^{\star}_{exit} = \tau_{LE}$), the series A investor's payoff depends on the optimal conversion decision of the group of Preferred Holders. If the investors as a group decide to convert, the Series A investor is obliged to convert as well and receives his pro-rata share of proceeds. If they decide *not* to convert, the series A investor receives his payoff from the chooser option generated by Liquidation Preference in interaction with Optional Conversion. Accordingly, he obtains either the liquidation amount or his pro-rata share of the proceeds remaining after payout of all Liquidation Preferences to his co-investors (see Section 3.1.4).

4 Application of the Pricing Model

This chapter presents an application of the contract pricing model developed in Chapter 3 to standard investment scenarios, which reflect alternative degrees of investor protection. In Sections 4.1 and 4.2, the author specifies the individual contract terms and shows how they can be combined to build full contracts. In Section 4.3, she presents and interprets the results from the LSM simulation.

4.1 Specification of Contract Terms

This section specifies the *price terms* and *non-price terms* of VC transactions.

4.1.1 Specification of Price Terms

The price terms of the series A financing are specified as follows:

- Pre-money valuation of the company (fully diluted):
  $V_{pre}(t_0) = \$16\text{m}$;

- Size of the series A financing (paid out in one installment at the investment date): $I_{vc_1}(t_0) = I_{VC}(t_0) = \$4$m;
- Price per share: $P(t_0) = \$10$.

Hence, the remaining dependent variables at t_0 are specified as follows:

- Post-money valuation (fully diluted):
  $V_{post}(t_0) = V_{pre}(t_0) + I_{vc_1}(t_0) = \$20$m;
- Total number of shares (fully diluted): $N^c_{tot}(t_0) = N^p_{tot}(t_0) = 2$m;
- Ownership percentage of the series A investor at t_0:
  $\alpha(t_0) = \beta(t_0) = 20\%$.

Furthermore, the exit dates (as agreed upon by the series A investor and company management) are defined as follows:

- Anticipated exit date: $t_{ant} = 6$ years;
- Latest possible exit date: $t_{max} = 8$ years.

The number and timing of future financing rounds and the respective price terms are determined by the jump process derived in Chapter 2.3. The participants in each follow-on round include all existing investors as well as one new (external) investor per round, in accordance with the model assumptions.

4.1.2 Specification of Non-price Terms

To specify the legal provisions, the author differentiates between two types of provisions: *basic* terms (and specifications), which are included in VC contracts by default because they represent the minimum level of protection acceptable to investors, and *negotiable* terms (and specifications), which are subject to negotiation between the parties. Whereas both types of terms are used to build the pricing scenarios, the assessment of *economic value* is performed only for negotiable terms.

4.1.2.1 Basic Terms

The basic terms include the following terms and specifications:

- **Simple Liquidation Preference**

  The VC investor is granted a simple liquidation preference, without participation and without multiple.

- **Optional Conversion**

  The Optional Conversion right is exercised only in the context of an exit event in the form of a Liquidation Event or Company Sale (see Section 3.1.3); the decision to convert is taken individually (and either aligned with the collective decision of the group of preferred holders or not).

- **Mandatory Conversion**

  This clause is triggered exclusively by the occurrence of a Qualified Public Offering (and not by a majority decision of preferred holders); since the IPO threshold level in the model exceeds the minimum conditions for a QPO (as explained in Section 3.1.1), any jump in valuation above the threshold level triggers the Mandatory Conversion of preferred shares.

- **Piggyback Registration**

  The investor has the right to piggyback on any registrations initiated by the company or the other investors (see Section 3.1.1).

- **Preemption Right**

  The investor is assumed to fully exercise his Preemption rights at each new financing round to avoid percentage dilution of his investment (see Section 3.2.3).

4.1.2.2 Negotiable Terms

The negotiable terms are derived from the Fenwick & West dataset. Table 5 shows the frequencies of terms and specifications by series of preferred stock, averaged over the five-year observation period from 2003 to 2008. According to these findings, the series A investor is nearly always granted a liquidation preference with participation (either capped or full participation). In the majority of cases, he is also provided with Anti-dilution protection. Demand Registration also represents a standard term in U.S. contracts, although it is not covered in the Fenwick & West dataset.[1] On

[1] This was confirmed by Michael Patrick (Fenwick & West).

the contrary, Redemption rights and Dividend rights are found only in a minority of cases and will not be included into the model scenarios in this chapter.

Additionally, the dataset shows that the most frequent terms remain unchanged across series, except for the seniority of Liquidation Preferences. More specifically, Liquidation Preferences are typically *pari passu* to existing Preferences in series B and C, while they are *senior* in financings of series D onwards. All other rights granted to VC investors in follow-on rounds (defined as financings of series B or higher) are the same as those granted to the series A investor.

Table 5: Frequency of Terms and Specifications by Series

	Series A	Series B				Series C				Series D				Series E+				Total Sample			
Provision / Specification	Total	Down	Even	Up	Total	Down	Even	Up	Total	Down	Even	Up	Total	Down	Even	Up	Total	Down	Even	Up	Total
Liquidation Preference																					
Seniority																					
Pari Passu	n/a	46%	44%	74%	67%	35%	35%	65%	56%	20%	25%	53%	40%	25%	39%	49%	39%	32%	36%	65%	54%
Senior	n/a	54%	56%	26%	33%	65%	65%	35%	44%	80%	75%	47%	60%	75%	61%	51%	61%	68%	64%	35%	46%
Multiple (if senior)																					
m <= 1x	n/a	74%	73%	93%	86%	78%	75%	87%	82%	72%	50%	86%	74%	70%	58%	90%	76%	73%	63%	89%	80%
1x < m <= 2x	n/a	21%	24%	7%	12%	15%	22%	13%	15%	26%	34%	13%	21%	21%	19%	9%	16%	21%	25%	10%	16%
m > 2x	n/a	4%	3%	1%	2%	7%	3%	0%	3%	3%	16%	1%	4%	10%	23%	1%	9%	6%	11%	1%	4%
Participation																					
Yes	59%	79%	73%	58%	62%	72%	76%	60%	64%	78%	65%	65%	69%	75%	73%	61%	68%	76%	71%	60%	65%
No	41%	21%	27%	42%	38%	28%	24%	40%	36%	22%	35%	35%	31%	25%	27%	39%	32%	24%	29%	40%	35%
Cap (if participating)																					
No	60%	49%	71%	50%	52%	44%	68%	50%	51%	60%	70%	49%	55%	64%	59%	52%	58%	54%	67%	50%	53%
Yes	40%	51%	29%	50%	48%	56%	32%	50%	49%	40%	30%	51%	45%	36%	41%	48%	42%	46%	33%	50%	47%
Anti-dilution																					
Protection																					
Yes	96%	98%	100%	99%	99%	96%	98%	99%	98%	100%	96%	98%	99%	98%	100%	97%	98%	98%	99%	99%	99%
No	4%	2%	0%	1%	1%	4%	2%	1%	2%	0%	4%	2%	1%	2%	0%	3%	2%	2%	1%	1%	1%
Formula																					
Weighted Average	98%	96%	88%	97%	96%	94%	88%	97%	96%	85%	82%	96%	91%	87%	86%	96%	91%	91%	86%	97%	94%
Full Ratchet	2%	4%	12%	3%	4%	6%	13%	3%	4%	15%	18%	4%	9%	13%	14%	4%	9%	9%	14%	3%	6%
Redemption																					
No	77%	66%	56%	78%	74%	66%	71%	74%	72%	69%	69%	73%	71%	74%	59%	76%	72%	69%	63%	76%	73%
Yes	23%	34%	44%	22%	26%	34%	29%	26%	28%	31%	31%	27%	29%	26%	41%	24%	28%	31%	37%	24%	27%
Dividends																					
No	96%	95%	90%	96%	95%	95%	98%	95%	95%	89%	90%	93%	92%	92%	82%	96%	92%	93%	90%	95%	94%
Yes	4%	5%	10%	4%	5%	5%	2%	5%	5%	11%	10%	7%	8%	8%	18%	4%	8%	7%	10%	5%	6%

Note: The frequencies are mean values over the time period 2004-2008, derived from the Fenwick & West dataset.

Based on these findings, the negotiable terms (and specifications) are defined as follows:

- **Liquidation Preference**

  This provisions has three alternative specifications based on the type of Participation: *No* Participation, *Capped* Participation (with the cap set at three times the initial investment) and *Full* Participation. The preferences are defined as pari passu preferences in financings of series A to C and as senior preferences in financings of series D onwards.

- **Anti-dilution Protection**

  This provision has three alternative specifications: *absence* of Anti-dilution protection, *weighted-average* Anti-dilution and *full-ratchet* Anti-dilution; in the weighed-average formula, the number of shares outstanding is defined according to the broad-based interpretation (accounting for all shares outstanding on a fully diluted basis).

- **Demand Registration**

  There are two alternative specifications: *absence* of Demand Registration and *presence* of Demand Registration (with initial date set equal to t_{ant}).

4.2 Specification of Base Scenarios

As explained in Section 2.2, the starting point for the pricing of embedded options is the specification of a base contract, that is of the combination of terms included in the contract under analysis. Practitioners would derive the base scenario directly from the Term Sheet, which sets out the initial terms and represents the starting point of negotiations. In this numerical experiment, however, the author uses model-type base scenarios, which are closely aligned with the NVCA model document and reflect different levels of investor protection. She defines three alternative base scenarios:

- Company-favorable scenario: contains only the basic legal terms.
- Middle-of-the-Road scenario: contains the basic legal terms as well as a Liquidation Preference with *full* participation, *weighted average* Anti-dilution and Demand Registration.
- Investor-favorable scenario: contains the basic legal terms as well as a Liquidation Preference with *full* participation, *full ratchet* Anti-dilution and Demand Registration.

4.3 Simulation Results and Interpretation

The author performs Monte Carlo simulations over 5,000 sample paths for each base scenario and for each alternative scenario (required to obtain option values of individual terms, as described in Section 2.2.3). The results for the individual base scenarios are presented in Tables 6 to 8. A comparison of the results across all base scenarios is provided in Table 9.

Table 6: Simulation Results for the Company-favorable Base Scenario

	Liquidation Preference			Anti-dilution Protection			Demand Registration	
	No Part.	Capped Part.	Full Part.	No Prot.	WA	FR	No	Yes
Base Scenario	X			X			X	
Contract Value	4.854.488	5.475.138	6.093.057	4.854.488	5.109.063	7.184.470	4.854.488	4.822.820
% change from base case	-	+12,79%	+25,51%	-	+5,24%	+48,00%	-	-0,65%
Term Value	0	620.650	1.238.569	0	254.575	2.329.982	0	-31.669
in % of contract value	-	11,34%	20,33%	-	4,98%	32,43%	-	-0,66%
Share of Proceeds	31,29%	33,40%	33,60%	31,29%	31,51%	32,61%	31,29%	31,27%
% change from base case	-	+6,74%	+7,39%	-	+0,71%	+4,22%	-	-0,05%
Eff. Company Value	16.394.370	15.102.773	14.899.460	16.394.370	16.164.087	15.264.605	16.394.370	16.401.166
% change from nom. value	-18,03%	-24,49%	-25,50%	-18,03%	-19,18%	-23,68%	-18,03%	-17,99%

Note: This table shows the simulation results for the company-favorable base scenario; in this scenario, the VC investors hold a Liquidation Preference without participation and are granted neither Anti-dilution protection nor Demand Registration rights. "Contract Value" reflects the option value of the full contract from the perspective of the series A investor. "Term Value" reflects the option value of an individual term; it is provided as an absolute value (that is as the difference between contract value *with* and *without* the term under analysis) and as a relative value (that is as a percentage of full contract value). The "Share of Proceeds" is defined as the series A investor's expected share of total exit proceeds (with total proceeds equaling the fully-diluted company valuation at exit). "Eff. Company Valuation" is the *effective* post-money valuation of the portfolio company at t_0. The "% change from nominal value" is the deviation of effective valuation from nominal valuation, which equals \$20m by assumption.

Table 7: Simulation Results for the Middle-of-the-Road Base Scenario

	Liquidation Preference			Anti-dilution Protection			Demand Registration	
	No Part.	Capped Part.	Full Part.	No Prot.	WA	FR	No	Yes
Base Scenario			X		X			X
Contract Value	5.077.093	5.709.135	6.326.496	6.062.143	6.326.496	8.293.867	6.357.689	6.326.496
% change from base case	-19,75%	-9,76%	-	-4,18%	-	+31,10%	+0,49%	-
Term Value	0	632.042	1.249.403	0	264.353	2.231.723	0	-31.193
in % of contract value	-	11,07%	19,75%	-	4,18%	26,91%	-	-0,49%
Share of Proceeds	31,50%	33,61%	33,82%	33,58%	33,82%	35,07%	33,84%	33,82%
% change from base case	-6,87%	-0,62%	-	-0,71%	-	+3,69%	+0,06%	-
Eff. Company Value	16.169.562	14.926.412	14.723.207	14.909.227	14.723.207	13.978.258	14.714.858	14.723.207
% change from nom. value	-19,15%	-25,37%	-26,38%	-25,45%	-26,38%	-30,11%	-26,43%	-26,38%

Note: This table presents the results for the middle-of-the-road base scenario, in which VC investors hold a Liquidation Preference with full participation, weighted average Anti-dilution protection and Demand Registration rights. "Contract Value" reflects the option value of the full contract from the perspective of the series A investor. "Term Value" reflects the option value of an individual term; it is provided as an absolute value (i.e. the difference between contract value *with* and *without* the term under analysis) and as a relative value (i.e. as a percentage of full contract value). The "Share of Proceeds" is defined as the series A investor's expected share of total exit proceeds (with total proceeds equalling the fully-diluted company valuation at exit). "Eff. Company Valuation" is the *effective* post-money valuation of the portfolio company at t_0. The "% change from nominal value" is the deviation of effective valuation from nominal valuation, which equals \$20m by assumption.

Table 8: Simulation Results for the Investor-favorable Base Scenario

	Liquidation Preference			Anti-dilution Protection			Demand Registration	
	No Part.	Capped Part.	Full Part.	No Prot.	WA	FR	No	Yes
Base Scenario			X			X		
Contract Value	7.149.284	7.745.253	8.293.867	6.062.143	6.326.496	8.293.867	8.328.995	8.293.867
% change from base case	-13,80%	-6,61%	-	-26,91%	-23,72%	-	+0,42%	-
Term Value	0	595.969	1.144.583	0	264.353	2.231.723	0	-35.128
in % of contract value	-	7,69%	13,80%	-	4,18%	26,91%	-	-0,42%
Share of Proceeds	32,59%	34,82%	35,07%	33,58%	33,82%	35,07%	35,10%	35,07%
% change from base case	-7,07%	-0,71%	-	-4,24%	-3,56%	-	+0,09%	-
Eff. Company Value	15.269.902	14.183.097	13.978.258	14.909.227	14.723.207	13.978.258	13.972.006	13.978.258
% change from nom. value	-23,65%	-29,08%	-30,11%	-25,45%	-26,38%	-30,11%	-30,14%	-30,11%

Note: This table presents the results for the investor-favorable base scenario, in which VC investors are granted a Liquidation Preference with full participation, full ratchet Anti-dilution protection and Demand Registration rights. "Contract Value" reflects the option value of the full contract from the perspective of the series A investor. "Term Value" reflects the option value of an individual term; it is provided as an absolute value (i.e. the difference between contract value *with* and *without* the term under analysis) and as a relative value (i.e. as a percentage of full contract value). The "Share of Proceeds" is defined as the series A investor's expected share of total exit proceeds (with total proceeds equalling the fully-diluted company valuation at exit). "Eff. Company Valuation" is the *effective* post-money valuation of the portfolio company at t_0. The "% change from nominal value" is the deviation of effective valuation from nominal valuation, which equals \$20m by assumption.

Table 9: Comparison of Results from Alternative Contracting Scenarios

	Liquidation Preference			Anti-dilution Protection			Demand Registration	
	No Part.	Capped Part.	Full Part.	No Prot.	WA	FR	No	Yes
Company-favorable Base Scenario								
Terms in Base Scenario	X			X			X	
Contract Value	4.854.488	5.475.138	6.093.057	4.854.488	5.109.063	7.184.470	4.854.488	4.822.820
% change (compared to company-favorat	+0,00%	+12,79%	+25,51%	+0,00%	+5,24%	+48,00%	+0,00%	-0,65%
Term Value	0	620.650	1.238.569	0	254.575	2.329.982	0	-31.669
% change in contract value (with vs. with	-	+12,79%	+25,51%	-	+5,24%	+48,00%	-	-0,65%
Effective Company Value	16.394.370	15.102.773	14.899.460	16.394.370	16.164.087	15.264.605	16.394.370	16.401.166
% change (compared to nominal compan	-18,03%	-24,49%	-25,50%	-18,03%	-19,18%	-23,68%	-18,03%	-17,99%
Middle-of-the-road Base Scenario								
Terms in Base Scenario			X		X			X
Contract Value	5.077.093	5.709.135	6.326.496	6.062.143	6.326.496	8.293.867	6.357.689	6.326.496
% change (compared to company-favorat	+4,59%	+17,61%	+30,32%	+24,88%	+30,32%	+70,85%	+30,97%	+30,32%
Term Value	0	632.042	1.249.403	0	264.353	2.231.723	0	-31.193
% change in contract value (with vs. with	-	+12,45%	+24,61%	-	+4,36%	+36,81%	-	-0,49%
Effective Company Value	16.169.562	14.926.412	14.723.207	14.909.227	14.723.207	13.978.258	14.714.858	14.723.207
% change (compared to nominal compan	-19,15%	-25,37%	-26,38%	-25,45%	-26,38%	-30,11%	-26,43%	-26,38%
Investor-favorable Base Scenario								
Terms in Base Scenario			X			X		X
Contract Value	7.149.284	7.745.253	8.293.867	6.062.143	6.326.496	8.293.867	8.328.995	8.293.867
% change (compared to company-favorat	+47,27%	+59,55%	+70,85%	+24,88%	+30,32%	+70,85%	+71,57%	+70,85%
Term Value	0	595.969	1.144.583	0	264.353	2.231.723	0	-35.128
% change in contract value (with vs. with	-	+8,34%	+16,01%	-	+4,36%	+36,81%	-	-0,42%
Effective Company Value	15.269.902	14.183.097	13.978.258	14.909.227	14.723.207	13.978.258	13.972.006	13.978.258
% change (compared to nominal compan	-23,65%	-29,08%	-30,11%	-25,45%	-26,38%	-30,11%	-30,14%	-30,11%

Note: This table summarizes the simulation results obtained from the three base scenarios. To facilitate the comparison of results across scenarios, the ratio "% change from base" is replaced by "% change in contract value (with vs. without term)". This ratio reflects the percentage deviation of total contract value *with* the term under analysis from total contract value *without* the term under analysis.

In the company-favorable base scenario (see Table 6), the investment contract generates an aggregate value of \$4,854,488 for the series A investor. This value is substantially increased in the presence of participating liquidation preference and anti-dilution protection. More specifically, the addition of capped participation increases full contract value by 12.79%, while full participation increases it by 25.51%. The presence of Anti-dilution protection increases full contract value by 5.24% (for weighted average), respectively by 48.00% (for full ratchet), as compared to the base scenario without any protection mechanism.
In the middle-of-the-road base scenario (see Table 7), the full contract generates a value of \$6,326,496, which represents an increase of over 30% as compared to the company-favorable base scenario. Accepting a cap on participation would reduce this value by 9.76%, while completely giving up the participatory feature would reduce it by 19.75% (as compared to the base scenario with full participation). In terms of Anti-dilution protection, moving from the weighted average formula to the full ratchet formula would increase contract value by 31.10%, whereas giving up the protection would reduce contract value by 4.18% (as compared to the base scenario with weighed average protection).
Finally, in the investor-favorable base scenario (see Table 8), the investment contract generates a total value of \$8,293,867. This reflects an increase of over 70% as compared to the contract value in the company-favorable base scenario. Moving from full participation to capped par-

ticipation would decrease contract value by 6.61%, while giving up the participatory feature would imply a loss of 13.80% in contract value. Accepting an Anti-dilution protection based on the weighted average formula would reduce contract value by 23.72%, while completely giving up the Anti-dilution protection would reduce it by 26.91% (as compared to the base scenario of full ratchet protection).

In all three scenarios, the presence of Demand Registration has a minor and negative impact on contract value to the series A investor, which is not surprising in the light of the model assumptions. On the one hand, the ownership share of preferred holders equals 20% after the series A financing, and further increases by over 17% at any follow-on round. This implies that the combined ownership percentage of the group of preferred holders is expected to exceed 50% at the series D financing, while Demand Registration only becomes exercisable at the series E financing.[2] Hence, when Demand Registration becomes exercisable, the group of preferred holders already controls the type and timing of exit (via their control rights). On the other hand, the exercise decision for Demand Registration is not taken by the series A investor individually, but by the group of preferred holders. The optimal exercise policy of the group may diverge from the optimal exercise policy of the series A investor, which implies a loss in contract value for the series A investor.

---

[2] Since the initial date of Demand Registration is set equal to six years after the initial investment and the waiting time between two consecutive pricing events is on average 18 months, the right becomes exercisable on average at the fourth jump date, that is the date of the series E financing.

The results obtained for Anti-dilution rights substantiate the widespread criticism of the full ratchet protection. As explained in Section 3.2.2, this type of protection is rarely used by practitioners because it is highly penalizing to common holders, who have to bear alone the full cost of any reduction in company value. Effectively, the full ratchet protection generates disproportionately high value for the series A investor, since it increases full contract value by 37% to 48% (for the company-favorable and the investor-favorable scenarios, respectively).

Most importantly, the results show that there is considerable value in the structuring of VC contracts, since total contract values can be increased by up to 70% by amending exclusively the negotiable terms. Moreoever, they reiterate the relevancy of *effective valuation*, a concept of (implied) company valuation, which accounts for the distribution of proceeds at exit (and not only for the investor's ownership percentage at the date of investment, which represents current practice).[3] In the given base scenarios, the series A investor acquires an initial ownership percentage of 20% and fully participates in follow-on rounds, while his expected share of exit proceeds lies between 31.29% (in the company-favorable scenario) and 35.07% (in the investor-favorable scenario), in spite of economic dilution caused by new investors in follow-on rounds. This divergence between (a) ownership percentage and (b) expected share of exit proceeds can be accounted for in the price terms of the contract. Based on an initial investment of

[3] This concept of effective valuation is introduced in Woronoff & Rosen (2005a).

$4,000,000 and an initial ownership percentage of 20%, the *nominal* post-money valuation of the company is $20,000,000 (obtained by dividing the initial investment by the ownership percentage), whereas the *effective* valuation (obtained by dividing the initial investment by the expected share of proceeds) ranges between $16,394,370 (in the company-friendly base scenario) and $13,978,258 (in the investor-friendly scenario).

5 Conclusion

This chapter summarizes and interprets the findings of the thesis and provides suggestions for future scientific research.

5.1 Summary of the Findings

In this work, the author has devised an option pricing model to assess the economic value of VC contracts and individual contract terms. The model covers the majority of provisions included in U.S. model documents and accounts for interaction effects between these terms. It integrates multiple series of preferred stock issued to multiple investors over several rounds. The option pricing methodology is flexible enough to accommodate complex exotic features of embedded options, such as uncertain timing, path-dependencies and American exercise rights generated when VC investors gain control over the timing of the exit transaction. The underlying asset of embedded options is modeled as a jump process, which reflects the discontinuous adjustments in the value of investee companies upon new financing rounds and the exit transaction. The model parameters are derived from time series data and do not require subjective estimation.

By applying the model to standard investment scenarios, the author obtains numerical estimates of contract values. The results show that VC contracts generate considerable economic value, and that this value is strongly influenced by negotiable provisions. By obtaining more investor-favorable terms at the outset of his investment, the series A investor can increase his total contract value by up to 70% (as compared to the company-favorable base scenario). Hence, there is considerable value in the structuring of VC contracts. Moreover, since VC contract provisions generate non-linear payoff functions, the VC investor's expected share of proceeds at exit exceeds by far his ownership percentage at investment (that is by over 15% in the investor-favorable scenario). This deviation reiterates the relevancy of the concept of "effective valuation". Lastly, the results show that the values of individual terms are strongly influenced by the remaining terms in the contract. This confirms the importance of accounting for interaction effects and of treating VC contracts as option baskets.

This thesis provides a contribution to the nascent line of research on the economic value of VC contracts. The range of legal terms covered is extended to voting rights (on the shareholder and board levels) as well as "initiatory" exit rights (including demand registration rights, drag-along rights and redemption rights). The analysis accounts for the various interaction effects between individual provisions by modeling them using trigger events, chooser options and joint option ownership. It also accommodates multiple rounds with multiple investors and multiple series of preferred shares. The application of the model to standard contract terms provides first numerical estimates of contract values in the U.S. Practitioners can rely on this approach to evaluate alternative investment structures and optimize the outcome of contract negotiations using quantitative arguments.

5.2 Directions for Further Scientific Research

The contract pricing framework developed in this thesis could be extended along several dimensions. First, it could be complemented to allow for the assessment of contract values from the perspectives of other investors than the initial one (the series A investor). Secondly, it could be adapted to legal environments and contracting practices in other countries or regions, based on model legal documents and time series data applicable for the specific geography. Finally, it would be valuable to further explore *shared* option ownership in VC contracts by combining the discrete-time pricing approach developed in this thesis with complex games. This would facilitate the pricing of tag-along rights and rights of first refusal, which represent standard clauses of VC contracts, but remain largely uncovered in the scientific literature.

This framework can furthermore be employed in related fields of research on VC contract design. On the one hand, it can be used for the development of general optimality arguments, which would be based on economic contract value and valid across countries or regions. On the other hand, it can be employed to add a value-based dimension to empirical studies and to obtain numerical evidence on contract values in different countries. This would facilitate the comparison of VC contract design across countries as well as the direct testing of theoretical arguments.

A Chi-squared Goodness-of-Fit Tests

A.1 Chi-squared Goodness-of-Fit Test Applied to Distribution of Upward Jump Amplitudes

The probability distribution function providing the best approximation to the observed distribution of upward jump magnitudes can be obtained by testing $H_0 : Y_{x^u} \sim Wei(\gamma, 1)$ using a chi-squared goodness-of-fit test. First, divide the sample space into 5 cells, namely $A_1, \ldots, A_5$. Let $p_j = P[Y \in A_j]$ and let o_j denote the number of observations that fall into the j-th cell. Under H_0 the expected number in the j-th cell equals $1204p_j$. H_0 is rejected at the 10% significance level if

$$X^2 = \sum_{j=1}^{5} \frac{oj - ej^2}{e_j} > \aleph^2_{0.90}(2) = 4.61.$$

Table 10 shows the observed and expected frequencies for the chi-squared test of a Weibull distribution with $k = 1$ and $\gamma = 0.8582$. As $X^2 = 3.97$, H_0 cannot be rejected at the $\alpha = 0.10$ level of significance and it thus appears that the exponential distribution (Weibull distribution with $k = 1$)

fits well the magnitude of upward jumps.

Table 10: Frequencies of the Magnitude of Upward Jumps

Magnitude (in %)	≤ 20	≤ 160	≤ 180	≤ 200	> 200
Observed Frequencies (o_j)	251	789	31	25	108
Observed Probabilities (p_j)	0.21	0.66	0.03	0.02	0.09
Expected Frequencies (e_j)	250	767	39	31	117

A.2 Chi-squared Goodness-of-Fit Test Applied to Distribution of Downward Jump Amplitudes

To estimate the probability distribution function providing the best approximation to the observed distribution of downward jump amplitudes, a chi-squared goodness-of-fit test is applied to $H_0 : Y_{x^d} \sim U(n)$. $U(n)$ is defined as a discrete uniform distribution with n equaling the number of cells dividing the sample space ($n = 5$). Table 11 shows the observed and expected frequencies for the chi-squared test of a uniform distribution. Since $X^2 = 5.36 < \aleph^2_{0.90}(4) = 7.78$, H_0 cannot be rejected at the $\alpha = 0.10$ level of significance and it appears that the uniform distribution well fits the magnitude of downward jumps. If u is a value sampled from the standard uniform distribution, then the value $a + (b - a)u$ follows the uniform distribution parametrized by a (minimum value) and b (maximum value). Since the magnitude of downward jumps must be in the interval [0, 1], the minimum and maximum values of the uniform distribution are defined as $a = 0$ and $b = 1$.

Table 11: Frequencies of the Magnitude of Downward Jumps

Magnitude (in %)	≤ 20	≤ 40	≤ 60	≤ 80	> 80
Observed Frequencies (o_j)	76	73	96	74	72
Observed Probabilities (p_j)	0.19	0.19	0.25	0.19	0.18
Expected Frequencies (e_j)	78	78	78	78	78

References

Admati, A., & Pfleiderer, P. (1994). Robust financial contracting and the role of the venture capitalist. *Journal of Finance*, *49*(2), 371-402.

Anderson, R., & Sundaresan, S. (1996). Design and valuation of debt contracts. *Review of Financial Studies*, *9*(1), 37-68.

Ashkeboussi, R., Juan, C., & Olmos, F. (2007, March). Evaluation of international joint venture agreements: Real options in practice (case study). *International Journal of Business*, *12*(2).

Bagley, C., & Dauchy, C. (2008). *The entrepreneur's guide to business law* (3rd ed.). Mason, OH: Thomson West.

Baldwin, C. Y., & Meyer, R. F. (1979). Liquidity preference under uncertainty: a model of dynamic investment in illiquid opportunities. *Journal of Financial Economics*, *7*(2), 347-374.

Bascha, A., & Walz, U. (2001). Convertible securities and optimal exit decisions in venture capital finance. *Journal of Corporate Finance*, *7*, 285-306.

Bergemann, D., & Hege, U. (1998). Venture capital financing, moral hazard, and learning. *Journal of Banking and Finance*, *22*(6-8), 703-735.

Bergemann, D., & Hege, U. (2000). *The financing of innovation: Learning and stopping.* (Working paper, Yale University, ESSEC Business School and CEPR.)

Black, B., & Gilson, R. (1998). Venture capital and the structure of capital markets: banks versus stock markets. *Journal of Financial Economics*, *47*(3), 243-277.

Black, F., & Cox, J. (1976). Valuing corporate securities - some effects of bond indenture provisions. *Journal of Finance*, *31*(2), 351-367.

Black, F., & Scholes, M. (1973). The pricing of options and corporate liabilities. *Journal of Political Economy*, *81*(3), 637-659.

Boyle, P. (1977). Options: A Monte Carlo approach. *Journal of Financial Economics*, *4*(3), 323-338.

Brobeck Hale and Dorr. (2003). *Full ratchet: The trans-atlantic venture capital review* (Tech. Rep. No. 2).

Camp, J. J. (2002). *Venture capital due diligence: a guide to making smart investment choices and increasing your portfolio returns* (1st ed.). New York: Wiley.

Chemla, G., Habib, M. A., & Ljungqvist, A. (2004, July). *An analysis of shareholder agreements.* (Working Paper, UBC, CNRS, CEPR, University of Zurich, and NYU Stern School.)

Cohen, A. C. (1965, November). Maximum likelihood estimation in the Weibull distribution based on complete and on censored samples. *Technometrics*, *7*(4), 579-588.

Cossin, D., Leleux, B., & Saliasi, E. (2002, February). *Understanding the economic value of legal covenants in investment contracts: A real-options approach to venture equity contracts.* (Working paper, University of Lausanne, HEC.)

Cox, J., Ingersoll, J., & Ross, S. (1985). A theory of the term structure of interest rates. *Econometrica*, *53*, 385-467.

Dupoyet, B. V. (2004, October). *Asymmetric jump processes: Option pricing implications.* (Working paper, Florida International University.)

Ewens, M. (2009, March). *A new model of venture capital risk and return.* (Working paper, UCLA.)

Gamba, A. (2003, December). *Real options: a Monte Carlo approach.* (Working paper, University of Verona.)

Gompers, P. A. (1995). Optimal investment, monitoring, and the staging of venture capital. *Journal of Finance*, *50*(5), 1461-1489.

Gompers, P. A. (1996). Grandstanding in the venture capital industry. *Journal of Financial Economics*, *42*(1), 133-56.

Gompers, P. A., & Lerner, J. (1996). The use of covenants: An empirical analysis of venture partnership agreements. *Journal of Law and Economics*, *39*(2), 463-498.

Hammersley, J. M., & Handscomb, D. C. (1964). *Monte Carlo methods.* (1st ed.). London & New York: Chapman & Hall.

Harrison, J. M., & Kreps, D. M. (1979). Martingales and arbitrage in multiperiod securities markets. *Journal of Economic Theory*, *20*(3), 381-408.

Harrison, J. M., & Pliska, S. R. (1981). Martingales and stochastic integrals in the theory of continuous trading. *Stochastic Processes and their Applications*, *11*(3), 215-260.

Heath, D., Jarrow, R., & Morton, A. (1992). Bond pricing and the term structure of interest rates: A new methodology for contingent claims valuations. *Econometrica*, *60*(1), 77-105.

Ingersoll, J. E. (1977). A contingent-claims valuation of convertible securities. *Journal of Financial Economics*, *4*(3), 289-231.

Jung-Senssfelder, K. (2006). *Equity financing and covenants in venture capital: An augmented contracting approach to optimal german contract design*. Wiesbaden: Deutscher Universitäts-Verlag.

Kahn, H., & Marshall, A. W. (1953). Methods of reducing sample size in Monte Carlo computations. *Journal of the Operations Research Society of America*, *1*, 263-271.

Kaplan, S. N., & Strömberg, P. (2002a, December). *Characteristics, contracts, and actions: Evidence from venture capitalist analyses.* (Working paper, University of Chicago.)

Kaplan, S. N., & Strömberg, P. (2002b). Financial contracting theory meets the real world: An empirical analysis of venture capital contracts. *Review of Economic Studies*, *70*(2), 281-315.

Karoui, N. E., & Martellini, L. (2001, November). *Dynamic asset pricing theory with uncertain time-horizon.* (Working paper, USC Marshall School of Business.)

Klausner, M., & Litvak, K. (2001, July). *What economists have taught us about venture capital contracting.* (Working paper, Stanfort Law School.)

Kou, S. (2002). A jump-diffusion model for option pricing. *Management Science*, *48*(8), 1086-1101.

Kou, S., & Wang, H. (2001, September). *Option pricing under a double exponential jump diffusion model.* (Working paper, Columbia University and Brown University.)

Lerner, J. (1994). The syndication of venture capital investment. *Financial Management*, *23*(3), 16-27.

Longstaff, F. A., & Schwartz, E. S. (2001). Valuing American options by simulation: A simple least-squares approach. *The Review of Financial Studies*, *14*(1), 113-147.

Merton, R. C. (1973). Theory of rational option pricing. *The Bell Journal of Economics and Management Science*, *4*(1), 141-183.

Merton, R. C. (1974). On the pricing of corporate debt: The risk structure of interest rates. *Journal of Finance*, *29*(2), 449-470.

Merton, R. C. (1976). Option pricing when underlying stock returns are discontinuous. *Journal of Financial Economics*, *3*(1-2), 125-144.

National Venture Capital Association. (2010, June). *Model venture capital financing documents.* Retrieved June 6, 2010, from National

Venture Capital Association website: http://www.nvca.org/resources/model legal documents.

Nöldeke, G., & Schmidt, K. M. (1998). Sequential investment and options to own. *RAND Journal of Economics*, *29*(4), 633-653.

Pennings, E., & Lint, O. (1997). The option value of advanced R&D. *European Journal of Operational Research*, *103*(1), 83-94.

Ramezani, C. A., & Zeng, Y. (1998, December). *Maximum likelihood estimation of asymmetric jump diffusion processes: Application to security prices.* (Working paper, California Polytechnic and University of Missouri.)

Sahlman, W. A. (1990). The structure and governance of venture-capital organizations. *Journal of Financial Economics*, *27*(2), 473-521.

Schertler, A. (2001, December). *Venture capital contracts: A survey of the recent literature.* (Working paper, Kiel Institute of World Economics.)

Schwartz, E., & Moon, M. (2000). Rational pricing of internet companies. *Financial Analysts Journal*, *56*(3), 62-75.

Smith, G. (2005). The exit structure of venture capital. *UCLA Law Review*, *53*, 315-356.

Thomson Reuters. (2009). *Nvca yearbook 2009* (Tech. Rep.). National Venture Capital Association.

Trigeorgis, L. (1996). *Real options: Managerial flexibility and strategy in resource allocation*. Cambridge, MA & London: MIT Press.

Willner, R. (1995). Valuing start-up venture growth options. In L. Trigeorgis (Ed.), *Real options in capital investment: Models, strategies and applications* (p. 221-239). Westport, CT: Praeger.

Wilmerding, A. (2006). *Term sheets & valuations: A line by line look at the intricacies of term sheets & valuations* (1st ed.). Boston, MA: Aspatore.

Wilmott, P. (2006). *Paul wilmott on quantitative finance* (2nd ed.). Chichester, West Sussex, England: Wiley.

Woronoff, M. A., & Rosen, J. A. (2005a). Effective vs. nominal valuations in venture capital investing. *NYU Law & Business Journal*, *2*, 101-131.

Woronoff, M. A., & Rosen, J. A. (2005b). Understanding anti-dilution provisions in convertible securities. *Fordham Law Review*, *74*, 101-134.

MIX
Papier aus verantwortungsvollen Quellen
Paper from responsible sources
FSC® C105338

If you have any concerns about our products,
you can contact us on
ProductSafety@springernature.com

In case Publisher is established outside the EU,
the EU authorized representative is:
Springer Nature Customer Service Center GmbH
Europaplatz 3, 69115 Heidelberg, Germany

Printed by Libri Plureos GmbH
in Hamburg, Germany